FECKERS: 50 PEOPLE WHO FECKED UP IRELAND

JOHN WATERS

Illustrations by Aongus Collins

Constable • London

Constable & Robinson Ltd
3 The Lanchesters
162 Fulham Palace Road
London W6 9ER

www.constablerobinson.com

First published in the UK by Constable,
an imprint of Constable & Robinson Ltd, 2010

A copy of the British Library Cataloguing in
Publication data is available from the British Library

ISBN: 978-1-84901-442-7

Printed and bound in the EU

1 3 5 7 9 10 8 6 4 2

PEFC/16-33-111
CATG-PEFC-052
www.pefc.org

Contents

CONTENTS

CONTENTS

FECKERS

Introduction

Everyone in Ireland, at least everyone who knows anything, knows what a 'fecker' is. But few, put under pressure to define the term, could do more than produce a synonym or two: 'gobshite', 'chancer', 'bollox'.

The word 'feck' is obviously related to another much-employed f-word. In daily usage it often acts as an alternative, supplanting the coarser, harder impact of the other with a gentler, more ironic inflexion. So it has all the connotations attaching to its more ubiquitous brother-word, and yet seems somehow not just to be less splenetic, but also less angry, less condemnatory somehow. There is an irony about 'feck', while also, strangely, a deeper quality of contempt. A 'fucker' is someone for whom the speaker retains a degree of respect, whereas 'fecker' has a hint of dismissiveness about it.

But the word 'fecker' retains about its person *some* element of regard. There is a sense that the accused is, if not exactly admired, at least held in a somewhat exasperated tolerance. A 'fecker' is someone who may exhaust the patience but not entirely the affections. When the epithet is directed at some absent miscreant, a smile is always in the offing. When levelled fact-to-face, it is liable to provoke a wink or a grin.

The invitation to 'Feck off!' was used with abandon by Father

Jack in the comedy series *Father Ted*. And, although this has given rise to the idea that 'feck' is a uniquely Irish word, the etymology of the word traces it to various sources in Middle English, Scots English and Hiberno-English.

'Feck' is a verb with several distinct meanings. One meaning relates to an improper or precipitous departure, as in: 'He fecked off and left her to mind the babby herself.'

Another, not unrelated meaning, suggests the abandonment of some responsibility, commitment or endeavour, to 'throw something there'; because, it is to be inferred, it was not going well. For example: 'He fecked the whole thing there and fecked off.' More prosaically, 'feck' can also mean simply 'to throw'. 'He fecked the bicycle in the lake and fecked off.'

'Feck' also means 'to steal'. 'He fecked a load of apples out of me garden.' Or, as used by that fecker James Joyce in *A Portrait of the Artist as a Young Man*, 'They had fecked cash out of the rector's room.'

In everyday usage, however, the word 'feck' is often used as a general-purpose swear-word. To 'feck things up', then, means simply to make a mess, or a 'hames' of everything. This use of the word seems also, though it may be coincidence, not entirely unrelated to the concept of fecklessness.

Whatever way you look at it, Ireland has certainly been fecked up. Popular opinion might at the moment be disposed to argue that it has been 'fecked' in a quite literal sense – that certain individuals and interests have stolen the fruits of Ireland's hard-won struggle for autonomy and self-sufficiency. You could, without raising a sweat, come up with fifty names of people who might be deemed blameworthy in this literal sense.

But this would be monotonous and somewhat misleading. While it is true that, in the past decade or so, a considerable amount of what called itself entrepreneurial activity amounted to a form of theft, it is also true that the roots of this go much deeper. To simply trawl through the newspapers, therefore, and pluck out the most frequently used names of venal bankers, developers and their political cronies would be to suggest that all the present misfortune is of recent derivation.

The failure of Ireland was not unforeseeable, nor was it an accident. Contrary to the analysis being peddled on a daily basis by ideologues with axes to grind, it did not flow from the corruption of a few bankers and politicians. Such an analysis would suggest that all sins are financial ones, as if nothing that has happened of late has any roots or connection to patterns established in the past when, really, nothing that has happened lately was in any serious degree unpredictable on the basis of even the most cursory observation of the weave of Irish life through the last century.

But in itself the recent economic catastrophe should have been an opportunity to ask a number of questions. How much longer could we congratulate ourselves on the 'opening up' of Irish society, without acknowledging that 'opening up' also destroyed the taboos which preserve many of the understandings of human nature that define civilization? For how long could we continue to quantify only those aspects of our alleged modernization which had been agreed as unambiguously virtuous, while ignoring the creeping consequences? And for how long could we continue to disregard the ambiguities of virtually every aspect of what we term 'progress', even in the face of escalating breakdown and complication?

Our failure to ask these questions stemmed from Ireland's most fundamental and ominous flaw: a failure of self-understanding.

'Change' is one of the most over- and misused words in the lexicon of modern Ireland. All the time we are reminded of how much Ireland has changed since that or then; since de Valera's 'comely maidens dancing at the crossroads' speech, since we crossed the border into what is deemed 'modernity' in 1960, since the First Programme of Economic Expansion, since the Robinson presidency, and so on. Invariably, the implication is that change can only be for the better. The problem with the kind of progress so loudly and pervasively celebrated in this society for several decades is not that it has occurred, but that it has occurred without a great deal of thought being applied to the complexities that change inevitably brings.

The origins of this problem are located not at the scene of the car crash of recent years, but long before, embedded in the grain and groove of Irish life, thought and everyday reality. It is arguable that the roots of the present crisis run deep into history, in the long saga concerning the abusive relationship between Ireland and its nearest neighbour. Undoubtedly, many of the difficulties of modern Ireland are profoundly connected to the Famine of the 1840s, and the failure adequately to incorporate the full meaning of that experience into the national imagination.

The problems began with a failure of thought. The way we had come to think about ourselves was problematic, because, although we had no clear insight into this, we were thinking about ourselves upside down. We did not understand the most basic facts about ourselves – for example, that we had for a long time been enslaved and were now embarking on a project of freedom as though there were nothing to it except embracing and acting out the role of freedom. But because we had no sense of what freedom meant, our efforts were doomed by virtue of a disastrous mimicry of things that did not suit us. The Irish became a nation of copycats, in which imitation was indicative of the highest form of intelligence we recognized.

There was a simple reason for this: it was how we had been

conditioned by our history and the abusive relationship that characterized that history. In order to be fully human, we had been led to understand, we needed to become as unlike ourselves as possible. A long time ago, we had been told – and had believed – that a nation of savages such as ourselves could never come to much. Our only hope was to emulate our abusers. Dependency suited our natures. It was our destiny. Even in freedom, we could not escape these facts of life.

The continuing avoidance of this self-awareness also made it essential that we did not think too deeply. Excessive self-reflection might lead us to gaze into the true nature of our history, and this might occasion a psychic reaction that would be impossible to predict or control. It was better, then, that we think about things at only the most superficial levels, and find ways of policing the thinking of our countrymen wherever possible. This is why almost everything that is said at a public level in Ireland is some kind of knee-jerk reaction against the most immediate interpretation of the most superficial facts. Nobody looks to history, to a deeper understanding of patterns that might still be holding Irish society in their grip.

This collection, in an attempt to shine a light on those patterns still evident in Irish society, will concentrate on the period, and people, of Ireland's independence, essentially the near-century since the final drive for sovereignty was started by the Easter Rising of 1916. A few figures pre-date this period, but usually because of some residual influence to be detected in the Ireland of today. If we are to discuss the entity that is present-day Ireland, it is to these 'feckers' we look in order to define our collective life and endeavours as a free nation. For these, I would argue, are the feckers who fecked up Ireland in as many ways as there are definitions of the word.

1 Padraig Pearse

Perhaps something most people in Ireland can agree upon, albeit for a host of different and often contradictory reasons, is that the undoing of national independence probably began with its genesis in the Easter Week of 1916. There is a school of thought, for example, holding that the Easter Rising was a misconceived folly, a pre-emptive strike that sought to achieve by force what was already in train. There is even a view – a ludicrous view, to put it frankly – that the Rising was an unwarranted attack on Irish 'democracy', being at the time unapproved by a majority of the people in the occupied Dublin of the time.

More recently, Padraig Pearse and the other leaders of 1916 have been blamed for the outbreak of conflict in the north of Ireland in the late 1960s – a few years after the fiftieth anniversary celebrations of the Rising in 1966. It should go without saying, of course, that the 1969 uprising in the North did not occur as a result of northern nationalists rediscovering their myth of destiny, but because a relatively small group of protestors, seeking to draw attention to the wholesale discrimination against Catholics in Northern Ireland, had been brutally stamped upon by the unionist establishment.

Latter-day analyses of Ireland's historical condition mostly agree that they blame 1916 for everything that came after it, while extending no credit for its achievement and no consideration of the fact that none of the leaders was in a position to control what happened afterwards.

Padraig Pearse has become a much caricatured figure in modern Ireland, his understanding of the nature of freedom being largely unappreciated by those who inherited the benefits. This vision is to be found in many of Pearse's poems – now disparaged by the modern literati – and other writings. In a series of essays written not long before the Rising, for example, Pearse outlined in detail the specifications of true independence, and the process by which it would be attained. The essays are rigorous and clear, and leave very little room for ambiguity about what the author saw as being necessary.

In one of these, 'The Murder Machine', about the effects of the English education system in Ireland, Pearse outlined the precise nature of the psychological effects of the colonial process. This was some fifty years before the groundbreaking works of the great Caribbean-born psychiatrist Frantz Fanon, who exposed the interior workings of the colonial machine in his classic works about the effects of French colonialism in Algeria.

Pearse perceived that the 'murder machine' had, in effect, created in Ireland the conditions of slavery. English rule in Ireland, he contended, had 'aimed at the substitution for men and women with "Things". It has not been an entire success. There are still a great many thousand men and women in Ireland. But a great many thousand of what, by way of courtesy, we call men and women, are simply Things. Men and women, however depraved, have kindly human allegiances. But these Things have no allegiance. Like other Things, they are for sale.'

True independence, Pearse wrote in another essay, 'The Spiritual Nation', 'requires spiritual and intellectual independence as its basis, or it tends to become unstable, a thing resting merely on interests which change with time and circumstances'.

He and the other leaders of the 1916 Rising were clear that the project of Independence must be a spiritual and psychological, as much as a political or cultural, process. Like Fanon, they intuited that only a superficial understanding of this necessary transformation could result in a disaster. But, following their execution, such elevated notions were replaced with more mundane understandings.

Without these deeper insights, everything seems simple: surely you simply undo what has been done to you? It takes a long time to perceive that such undoing is impossible without causing everything to unravel. The indigenous culture, having been interrupted, lacks a definitive sense of its own nature or direction. It still exists, but in an altered form, and cannot simply be decontaminated and reconditioned for a new phase of existence. The collective mindset is affected by a series of paradoxical conditions. On the one hand, there is a desire to purge everything alien; on the other, there is the unavoidable fact that the mindset itself has been infiltrated by alien influences, the most insidious of which is a tendency to imitate. The native wishes to redefine himself, not merely in contradistinction to his historical abuser, but in a manner that will bear witness to his authentic self; and yet, this authentic self can no longer be located, because it has been altered by the influence of the colonizer, whom the native has been conditioned to perceive as the most worthy subject of emulation. The native has been convinced, unbeknownst to himself, that his authentic self is a worthless thing, and that his only salvation resides in imitating his master, whom, at a conscious level, he imagines himself to despise. Who, then, is in charge? What is the nature of authenticity? What is to be made of the liberated native's determination to again become 'himself', if his sense of direction is provided by the indoctrination he has received?

Such understandings of the scale of the task that lay ahead were lost to the work of the firing squads. Thus, the very moments that provoked the surge towards freedom also began its undoing. The momentum was created but the intelligence that had already defined the freedom project not as a political or economic process, but as a spiritual rebirthing and a psychological recasting, was lost. What remained was the crudest understanding of what required to be done. The inevitable outcome was a failure of intellectual and psychological reintegration, which spawned a mishmash of confused and inauthentic identities. On the one hand, driven by the unattainable desire for a reclaimed authenticity, there began an era defined by protectionism and backlash, a ritualistic purging of everything 'alien' and, therefore, false. At the other extreme, governed by the self-hatred inculcated by the colonizer, there developed a repugnance and mistrust of everything indigenous. Most of this remains unresolved.

The first, perhaps the most enduring, catastrophe of independent Ireland, then, is that all the thought, all the insight that had inspired those who led the burst for freedom, ended up in pools of blood in the yard of Kilmainham Gaol. In getting themselves shot, Pearse and the other great leaders of 1916 denied posterity the intelligence they might have brought to the independence project, and instead left Ireland to the tender mercies of the literalists and crawthumpers who had been far too cunning to fall foul of firing squads.

2 Maud Gonne

Major John MacBride, executed for his part in the Rising of Easter Week 1916, is remembered mainly by his characterization by W.B. Yeats in the poem 'Easter 1916' as a 'drunken vainglorious lout'. These three words have come to outweigh the glories and sacrifices of his life and death. There are many lies in Irish poetry, but this is probably the worst.

Until recently, accounts of the domestic conflict between MacBride and his wife, Maud Gonne, which gave rise to the Yeats smear, told an entirely one-sided version of events. In the course of divorce and custody proceedings arising from the breakdown of their disastrous marriage, Gonne accused MacBride of drunkenness, cruelty, violence, infidelity and immorality. In addition to Yeats's writings, published accounts of their relationship by historians and biographers, infatuated beyond reason or fairness by the Yeats legend, repeated the prejudices and untruths arising from Gonne's version and Yeats's determination to believe it.

Not until Anthony J. Jordan's 2000 book, *The Yeats-Gonne-MacBride Triangle*, did Major MacBride's side of the story become widely available, and this has been largely ignored. Jordan undertook the simple endeavour of visiting the National Library of Ireland to read Major MacBride's papers, bequeathed to the State by the family with whom MacBride had been staying before his

death. The content of these is interrogative of any sense of complacency we may have about what we have come to 'know' about history and how we 'remember' the three pivotal Irish figures comprising this triangle.

The immorality charges, including the allegation that MacBride indecently molested his wife's eleven-year-old daughter, Iseult Gonne, and committed adultery with her half-sister, eighteen-year-old Eileen Wilson, are rebutted in MacBride's version. By his own admission, marrying Gonne was foolish. 'I gave her a name that was free from stain and reproach and she was unable to appreciate it once she had succeeded in inducing me to marry her.' Gonne became pregnant soon after their wedding in Paris in 1903 and gave birth in January 1904 to a son, Seaghan, later Sean MacBride, the eminent IRA chief of staff, lawyer and human rights activist. Major MacBride was determined his son should grow up in Ireland, but his wife had other ideas. She issued MacBride with an ultimatum: either he would admit the charge of indecency, renounce rights to his son and emigrate to America, or he would face an action for criminal assault.

There is every indication that, far from the injured heroine of popular mythology, Maud Gonne was a cunning manipulator, who, on deciding to divorce her husband, manufactured the evidence to banish him not just from her own life but also from that of his son, using Yeats as her Chief Minister of Propaganda. Yeats had an obvious vested interest in condemning MacBride: he was in love with Gonne and devastated by her marriage.

In the ensuing divorce proceedings in Paris, a close friend and confidante of Maud Gonne's gave evidence on behalf of MacBride, saying Gonne had spoken to her in the warmest terms of her husband just weeks before the proceedings began. To one charge, that of sexual assault on a cook, MacBride responded: 'If I wanted a woman I had plenty of money in my pocket and would have no difficulty in making a suitable choice in Paris, without trying to rape a hideously ugly old cook in my wife's house.' A midwife said she had seen MacBride 'kissing' Eileen Wilson, with whom MacBride said he had never been alone in the house. Of a servant who claimed to have found sperm marks on Eileen Wilson's bedclothes, MacBride declared: 'It is incomprehensible how this woman (an unmarried woman) can swear positively, as she does, that the marks on Eileen Wilson's linen were spots of sperm.' MacBride also pointed out that Eileen Wilson and Iseult Gonne slept in the same room. Of the incident in which he was alleged to have sexually assaulted Iseult, he says that she burst into his room one morning when he had 'the chamber pot in [his] hand'.

The court rejected the immorality charges against MacBride, accepting only one charge of drunkenness. Maud Gonne was awarded sole guardianship of Seaghan, with John entitled to visiting rights every Monday at the home of the mother. Heartbroken at the outcome, MacBride exercised his visiting rights on a couple of extremely tense occasions, and eventually returned to Dublin. He would never see his son again. Gonne, in a calculated effort to distance Seaghan from his father, insisted that his first language be French; thus Sean MacBride's lifelong hallmark French accent.

Major MacBride's involvement in the Rising appears to have been accidental. He was not a member of the formal republican leadership, his military distinction arising mainly from his formation of the Irish Brigade to assist the Boers in 1900. He told his court martial on 4 May 1916 that he had left his lodgings in Glenageary on the morning of Easter Monday, and gone into town to meet his brother, who was coming to Dublin to get married. On St Stephen's Green, he saw a band of Irish Volunteers, who told him that a Republic was about to be declared. 'I considered it my duty to join them,' he said. He was made second-in-command of a battalion at Jacob's factory.

MacBride was sentenced to death on 4 May and shot the following morning.

Kevin Christopher Higgins, in a poem about the execution, 'How He Died', quoted words attributed to MacBride addressing his firing squad: 'Let you rest well o' nights; myself will do it for one!/And tell them nobody cried!'

MacBride, a fearless and heroic soldier, went to his death the victim of what would only many decades later become known as parental alienation syndrome. Although his son was to become one of the central figures in the life of the Irish nation over the coming century, he referred to his father in public or in writing on only a couple of occasions, none of them any more than a perfunctory reference to a man for whom he appeared to have no store of affection. It is therefore perhaps appropriate that his mother, elevated by the poetry of one of the giants of world literature, has become an icon of a society in which, on a daily basis, mothers are enabled by the State to stand between fathers and children, and encouraged to see the next generation of Irish citizens as their own personal property.

3 Arthur Guinness

In 2009, Guinness celebrated its 250th anniversary with a load of hoo-hah and humbug. There were posters all over Dublin, allegedly the birthplace of the world-famous alcoholic drink, and advertising campaigns running in every medium inviting citizens to 'raise a glass to Arthur'. Newspapers who had profited much over the years from advertising campaigns by the company ran fawning articles and editorials paying tribute to 'the pint of plain'.

But 'stout' was actually invented not in Dublin, but in London, and was copied by Arthur Guinness when the standard ale he was purveying began to decline in popularity. Arthur Guinness's first brewery was in Leixlip, County Kildare, established in 1756, with a £100 inheritance from his godfather. He later passed on the business to his brother and in 1759 opened up a brewery in St James's Gate in Dublin. It would be several decades before Guinness began to brew stout. The word 'stout', incidentally, was also created in London, originally as an adjective to describe a dark ale called porter. Later on, it became the popular term for the drink.

It wasn't until much later that Guinness was spoken of as the Irish national drink. According to the historian Cormac O'Grada, it was only in the late nineteenth century, in the wake of the Famine, that 'stout' began to become popular outside the capital. A major factor in the success of the brand was the spread of temperance movements, which concentrated on spirits, viewing beer and stout as fairly harmless. But stout was still pretty slow to catch on, being regarded as somewhat unpleasant to taste and a poor substitute for the genuinely traditional poitín.

All this is intriguingly emblematic of the overall drift of Irish culture, which has 'traditionally' tended towards exaggerated notions of 'tradition', often investing enormous levels of enthusiasm in phenomena of doubtful progeny. It is interesting that the ancient Irish harp symbol was initially used as a symbol for Guinness, registered in 1876, and later adopted by the Irish Government as its official symbol. Nowadays, the multinational alcohol conglomerate Diageo, which has owned the Guinness brand since 1997, has its headquarters in London. Guinness is a global brand, with little more than a sentimental connection to its 'native' city.

Indeed, alcoholic beverages in general provoke in the Irish personality a particular form of sentimentality not directed at any other liquids. Water is taken for granted. Tea is patronized. Coffee, increasingly, is sneered at as an emblem of Celtic tiger excess. But a pint of plain, it seems, is still 'your only man'.

Yet, nobody doubts that our culture of alcohol consumption is unhealthy and damaging. Our rates of binge drinking – defined as drinking with the primary purpose of achieving intoxication – are several times higher than in most other countries, with the notable exception of our nearest neighbour. Half of Irish men and one-fifth of Irish women binge at least once a week. More than 100 Irish people die every month as a direct result of alcohol. The average Irish adult consumes twenty-one units of alcohol per week, the equivalent of more than ten pints, three bottles of wine or one bottle of spirits. When you consider that a significant proportion of Irish people – about one in five – do not drink at all, this figure becomes even more bloated.

When you get right down to it, the whole point of a glass of alcohol is to trick about with cognition. Guinness is not a squash or a soda – it is a liquid drug, a mind-altering concoction. The whole point of downing a pint is to do something to your mind – to reduce anxiety, to increase self-esteem, to shake off inhibitions, and in extreme cases, to achieve a temporary annihilation of the consciousness. A pint of Guinness has a certain iconic appearance, but really it amounts to a container of fluid exhibiting pharmacological properties calculated to relax, sedate, disinhibit or stimulate.

Perhaps we should be thinking more about our need for such a substance. Why should a culture choose to celebrate these objectives? Why do we take for granted that it is a good thing that so many of us use alcohol to loosen ourselves up and become more convivial, that drink liberates our vocal cords and enables us to talk more?

The same mind-altering process that relaxes and disinhibits is also the one that impairs judgement, destroys co-ordination, sparks explosive over-sensitivity, induces violent rages and sometimes leads people to arrive at such a dismal view of their existences that they take radical steps to annihilate themselves. The same product that we celebrate as 'part of what we are' is also what leads to unspeakable misery, madness and death.

Alcohol has many consequences the drinks companies prefer us not to think about: death, disease, violence, pain, mental incapacitation. Our culture is ignorant about the long-term damage to be traced in the emotional, psychological and social underdevelopment of people whose interior lives become frozen because of their use of alcohol as a crutch to get them through life.

Our culture has developed various stratagems to dispose of uncomfortable voices seeking to alert us to the abnormality of Irish drinking patterns. It is hazardous, in general company in Ireland, to say that you don't drink. Immediately, you have a sense of being different, and not just different as you might be if you admitted you didn't smoke or play golf, but different in that, in a quite fundamental sense, you do not belong. To be a non-drinker in Ireland without a 'good' excuse is to be a weirdo, possibly a religious nutcase, a health freak, or both.

The public house has long been for the Irish far more than a locus of conviviality and social interchange. It is really a parallel nation in which the emotional life of our society is played out. It is where we go to be completely ourselves. Drink is for the Irish not merely an instrument of sociability, but also a painkiller, an avoidance therapy, a licence to be free, a fumble for eternity, a substitute for faith in something higher. To be excluded from such essential (albeit unhealthy) rituals, even on a voluntary basis, is to suffer a great loss – to be barred from the collective soul of Ireland. It is in some ways only a minor consolation to know that you are missing also the pain and grief that nobody mentions in the drink ads.

For all these reasons, Arthur Guinness might have been a good businessman, but he makes for a dubious national hero.

4 Eamon de Valera

There are many things for which Eamon de Valera might plausibly be blamed. The thing is that he is nearly always blamed for the wrong things.

Dev was, undoubtedly, the leader of the 'second XV' who took to the field after the first team had been shot in the wake of the 1916 Rising. He subsequently led Ireland into a period of cultural introspection and economic isolation, with arguably catastrophic consequences in the continuance of emigration and the failure of the Irish economy to operate.

There is a delicious story of Dev at Croke Park in the 1950s – the darkest period of the Irish economy until 2008. Dev was throwing in the ball to start an important football fixture, when, in the silence that fell as the ball hung in the air, a voice rang out from the midst of the crowd: 'Good man, Dev, why not throw in your own two as well and make a pawnshop of the match like you have of the country?!'

Perhaps the greatest damage Dev did to his country, though, related not to his actions but his words, in particular the delivery, on St Patrick's Day 1943, of a speech that has come to define Ireland's sense of itself, albeit in a wholly negative way.

The speech, delivered in a radio broadcast on the national feast day, was really formulated to mark the fiftieth anniversary of the

founding of the Gaelic League, the organization which had, with a high degree of success, spearheaded the effort to restore the Irish language and native culture, and reawaken national self-confidence, following the disgrace and death of the great nationalist leader, Charles Stuart Parnell. The main theme of the speech was the importance of continuing the revival of the Irish language. Mr de Valera began his speech in Irish, and then continued in English.

'That Ireland which we dreamed of,' he intoned, 'would be the home of a people who valued material wealth only as the basis of right living, of a people who were satisfied with frugal comfort and devoted their leisure to the things of the spirit – a land whose countryside would be bright with cosy homesteads, whose fields and villages would be joyous with the sounds of industry, with the romping of sturdy children, the contests of athletic youths and the laughter of happy maidens, whose firesides would be forums for the wisdom of serene old age. It would, in a word, be the home of a people living the life that God desires that man should live.'

This passage is at once the most remembered and mis-remembered excerpt from what is certainly the most famous speech in recent Irish political history. Known as the 'Dream' speech, or the 'Comely Maidens' speech, or the 'Dancing at the Crossroads' speech, the hold it continues to have over the Irish imagination is extraordinary. For, in a sense, the entire edifice of modern Ireland is constructed as a reaction to everything that is contained in the passage quoted above.

As readers may already have noted, there is nothing in that passage about comely maidens, or dancing at the crossroads. And yet, most Irish people would stake their lives on the belief that it contains a mess of verbiage about both of these concepts. Although the phrase 'comely maidens' did appear in the official text, the recording of the speech as broadcast has Mr de Valera saying 'happy maidens'. But 'comely maidens' adds much more than 'happy maidens' to the caricature that successive generations have created out of the de Valera dream. And so, it has been necessary for us to 'forget' that Mr de Valera, before delivering his speech, drew his pen through the word 'comely' and replaced it with 'happy'. And, of course, Dev disobligingly appears to have omitted any reference to crossroads from this or any other oration.

The speech has been used, again and again, to summon up disrespect and contempt for the values to which de Valera was giving mere passing lip-service. Setting out to define what we might become, de Valera might in retrospect be said to have succeeded only in listing all the things we would no longer wish to be. As a result, the name of de Valera, mentioned in today's Ireland, provokes, almost invariably, snorts of derision. Anyone seeking to mount any serious criticism of the way Irish society has drifted into a ham-fisted version of modernity will eventually find themselves face to face with a caricature based on 'de Valera's Ireland', which they will allegedly be trying to rehabilitate.

Taken in context, for what it was, Dev's speech was an innocent product of its time. But appropriated in retrospect, by a different age, it became, with a little judicious tweaking, a highly effective weapon of derision. The result of all this is that everything Eamon de Valera ever uttered, stood for or dreamt about is now not simply taboo – it is downright wrong. The correct course in any given situation is therefore as near as possible to the opposite of whatever Dev might have proposed. And this, more than anything else, is what has led us into perdition.

De Valera became a kind of national scapegoat in our pursuit of modernization and prosperity. Because he embodied and represented so much of what we had been, he became a convenient symbol in the demolition of the past and the construction of a future that was eventually to disintegrate under our shoes. He was, of course, highly suitable in this regard. He was old, even when he was young. He was tall and austere and somewhat blind. He had a fascination with boring things, like history and mathematics. He was an archetypal father-figure, and therefore an easy target for Oedipal rage.

But he was, perhaps most importantly, a Catholic who had perceived the importance of spiritual cohesion to an emerging nation and had taken careful steps to stitch the ethos of Catholicism into the fabric of the State. Having evaded the firing squads of 1916, he lacked the complex vision of the revolutionaries who had died. He had a literal view of reality, and was given to flowery rhetoric without much substance.

Because he was such an easy target, he made the assault on pre-existing values much easier than it might otherwise have been. Everything he brought within his embrace – the land, frugality, community, even the family – became fair game in the ideological war that would dominate Irish culture for the last three decades of the twentieth century. By paying them homage in one speech, de Valera ensured that they too became easy targets for those who, inspired by the sibling revolution that had swept European universities in the late 1960s, had decided to kick Ireland into a new shape.

5 Rev. R.S. Devane S.J.

Fairly typical of the thinking that was to impel Ireland in a cultural direction contrary to its everyday reality was a once well-known Jesuit called R.S. Devane. Father Devane had an obsession with capturing and defining the essence of the Irish personality. He curiously (for a Catholic priest) seemed to be possessed of – or by – a characteristic that Patrick Kavanagh would elsewhere define as a 'Protestant' affliction: the curse of those who 'doubting that their Irishness would ooze, have put it on from the outside'. This outlook, declared the poet, 'is similar to the sentimental patriotism which takes pride – or pretends to take pride – in the Irishness of a horse that has won the Grand National, with the emphasis on the beast's Irishness instead of its horsiness'.

In 1950, Fr Devane produced a pamphlet, ostensibly about the pernicious influence of the British media, entitled 'The Imported Press'. He bemoaned the rising tide of British cultural forms – books, magazines, newspapers – 'appealing to children, to youth, to our women, to all classes, supplying to them the same mental pabulum as is supplied to the "Great British Public", now unfortunately so largely dechristianized as to need reconversion'.

The condescension of hindsight aside, Fr Devane's diatribe enables us to observe in clear form the nature of the cultural misunderstandings that beset our still young nation in the absence of clear thinkers with a complex awareness of how human cultures develop.

Devane seemed to take it for granted that there was some shimmering quantity of indigenous Irish culture which, if it could be corralled and purged of all alien influences, would initiate some magnificent resuscitation of the Irish mind. He appeared to have no sense whatever of the fact that, once changed by external influences, a culture has as much chance of returning to its prior state as a bell of being unrung.

In the most famous passage in 'The Imported Press', Fr Devane declared: 'A factor of deep significance in the recent evolution of our country has been the establishment of the Gaelic League in 1893. Only those of the older generation can adequately appreciate the dynamic influence of that movement in the first decade of this century. The soul of the nation was then deeply stirred by it. A mystic idealism spread throughout the land. A national messianism, the feeling that the nation had a sacred mission, took possession of the people. Ireland was on the point of realizing the long-dreamt hope of being "a nation once again". The widespread revival of Irish music, song and dance, and the language revival, gave ample proof of the dawning of a new day. The nation was one in ideal and in action.

'It is now sad to look back on those halcyon days, and to see the blight of the Civil War and the fratricidal strife that followed in its wake. Gone is the idealism; gone the mysticism; gone the messianism. They have been replaced by cynicism, fatalism and pessimism. Native music and song have given way to jazz, crooning and the dances of African primitives.'

In those paragraphs is contained a succinct summary of the thinking that was to result in far greater damage to the fabric of Irish culture than anything inflicted in the 800 years of invader sabotage. The Devane approach, which was identical to that which governed most official thinking about culture in the first half-century of independence, takes for granted that culture is to be located in the concrete evidence of an artefact, a dance step, an arpeggio, a sentence or a brushstroke. But of course the spirit of a culture derives not from objects, marks, movements or sounds, but from the life of a people. It is organic and spontaneous and is 'authentic' only when it reflects the life being lived at the moment of its generation. A correct analysis of Irish culture would have apprehended it as a complex, variegated organism comprising many diverse elements – some native, some English, some hybridized exoticisms that, by virtue of the uniqueness of the crucible of their formation, were capable of bestowing a new richness and self-understanding on the people.

Devane's error was to confuse tradition with traditionalism. For him the sum of Ireland's authentic, intrinsic identities could be captured by a process of purification. By harking backwards to some 'remembered' excellence that had existed prior to contamination by the 'alien', he believed the essence of Ireland could be rediscovered and rehabilitated. In this he was typical of a generation that considered itself to be adhering to the guidance of Padraig Pearse, while actually utterly misreading him. For not only was 'de-Anglicization' an impossible project; it was also a complete misunderstanding of how culture works. Pearse had never suggested that, in order to rediscover what was authentically 'Irish', it was necessary to cleanse it of elements that were 'unIrish' or 'not Irish'. On the contrary, he had insisted that the existence of any number of externally derived elements in the culture did not disqualify that culture from being understood as 'Irish', or even 'Gaelic'. His view of nationhood was based on that of Thomas Davis, the Protestant ideologue of the Young Ireland movement, who held that nationality was a spirituality, a power alive in the land, by which all those who lived in that land could become connected.

The defining problem with an arrested culture is that it has no way of growing organically, or even of imagining how this might have happened if the interruption to its growth had not occurred. A superficial understanding suggests just two ways of responding: fossilization, or a process of lurching forward in jumps and starts, reacting neurotically to developments elsewhere, imitating, rejecting and trying to unbecome what you have been given as a self-description.

Some post-colonial nations cope with these conditions better than others. Some simply throw their hats at the past, and move on to create its antithesis. Neither course is healthy, and either is doomed to provoke a backlash in the other direction.

The correct course requires a subtle understanding of the relationship between tradition and freedom. Tradition is merely the inherited hypothesis, which, being tested all the time, creates a tentative, provisional understanding of meaning. It is never definitive, never more than an ironic attempt at comprehension. And each attempt is alive only when the emotional reality that created it remains present also, and is free to interrogate tradition and reject it if necessary. Tradition should be respected but not revered to the point where it becomes the only consideration. Also to be considered is the freedom to re-create in the new conditions of the 'now'. In the absence of these conditions, art and culture become dead things, and the core misunderstandings set off a prolonged cultural reaction in which attempts at retrenchment are followed by outright repudiation. This phenomenon is at the core of the failure of independent Ireland. A crude choice was proffered: either the authentically pure or the uncomplicated other. Things could be

'Irish' or 'not Irish' but there could be no point of convergence. Thus, the process that should have led to self-understanding simply set off a series of reactions and counter-reactions in the cultural arena, while the authentic life of the re-emerging nation followed a course that, more and more, was not recognized as 'culture' at all.

6 Brendan Behan

Brendan Behan is one of Ireland's most famous writers, although he wrote only one good book and, by many accounts, had a minor role in a couple of plays that were to bear his authorial credit. Perhaps more to the point, his face adorns beer mats and brewers' crests in the 'literary' pubs of Dublin, alongside the Great Masters like Joyce, Beckett, Kavanagh and Yeats. His name brings a smile to the faces of tourists seeking to get in touch with the soul of Ireland.

Borstal Boy is a moderately good book. It is funny and touching and displays to good effect the author's sharp ear for dialogue. It offers the promise of a talent yet to flower but scant evidence to support the myth of Brendan Behan, which has endured for half a century while the works of better and far more prolific writers have faded from memory.

Had Behan not been a hellraiser, a drunk, a boor and a bollox, it is doubtful if anyone would remember him now. *Borstal Boy* would occasionally turn up in bargain bins. On the other hand, had he not been a hellraiser, a drunk, a boor and a bollox, he might well have written many more good books, even perhaps a few great ones. He was, by some accounts, a sensitive man, who could speak, it is said, French. But Patrick Kavanagh, who managed to combine a lifestyle of dissolution with the creation of a body of work that ranks

alongside that of the greatest writers Ireland has produced, described Behan as 'evil incarnate'.

Behan's influence on Irish literature has been almost entirely negative. The myth of Brendan Behan suggests that drinking and literature go hand in hand – indeed, that they are the same thing. In no other country in the world would Behan be remembered as a great writer. People might reflect on the tragedy of his life, and the scandal of a promising talent gone to seed, but nobody would regard a book and a couple of middling plays as a sufficient oeuvre to justify claims of genius and greatness. In Ireland Behan is remembered not merely as a literary genius but also as a scintillating wit, who, it seems, was wont to deliver himself of lines like 'Fuck the begrudgers!' with effortless facility and aplomb.

In his book *In My Own Time: Inside Irish Politics and Society*, James Downey described the Behan he knew in the Dublin of the 1950s. Though an admirer of his published writing, he wrote, it was difficult to admire Behan as a human being. Downey described Behan as: 'a gurrier unwashed, violent, delighting in every kind of misbehaviour, lazy, an abuser of his marvellous talents, and, worst, mean-spirited.' He recalled the literary collossus in his final days swaggering from pub to pub, accompanied by hangers-on, ignoring his old friends, flaunting cheques from American publications for writings into which he had put minimum effort.

In Downey's portrait it is possible to perceive something of the truth about Behan, including an explanation for his failure as a writer and success as a literary legend. According to Downey, Behan's hugely successful play *The Hostage* was written chiefly by Joan Littlewood. *The Quare Fellow* was rewritten from the beginning by Carolyn Swift 'from what amounted to no more than raw material supplied to her by Behan'. Swift staged the play at the Pike theatre, which she ran with her husband, Alan Simpson.

Downey recalled that, when the play was eventually produced at the Abbey, Behan went on stage afterwards and made a drunken curtain speech in which he said that the Abbey production was the definitive version, making no mention of Swift and all the work she had done. 'I thought that unforgivable,' Downey concluded.

Much worse, however, is the legacy Behan bequeathed Irish society concerning the very idea of The Writer. Out of his flimsy catalogue of works there developed a myth that grows all the while. The myth of Behan created the literary bore to be found in landmark Dublin pubs like Davy Byrne's and McDaids, a wet-brained, dandruffed species whose garrets might be imagined to strain at the seams with works of genius that nobody has the courage to publish. These inheritors of Behan seem not to have understood that, in order to qualify as a 'writer', it is somewhat important to have written and published books. Nor does it occur to any of these prodigies that anything of merit that their hero ever produced was conceived, if not actually written, while he was banged up for his activities as a 'patriot', or that the liberated Behan was a pretentious and self-aggrandizing writer, who worked only when the pubs were shut.

Yet these inheritors of the mantle of Brendan Behan remain unfazed and unapologetic about the dearth of evidence concerning their own 'genius'. All it takes, they tell themselves, is one great book. Behan is their inspiration and their patron saint, the validation they need for a lifestyle with not even the remotest connection to literary endeavour. They sit glowering over their pints, complaining about the begrudgers who seek to do them down, dropping references to their 'forthcoming' novels for the benefit of gullible tourists who wet themselves to be in the company of these successors to the great 'Broth of a Boy'. It is all unspeakably tedious, and lethal to any sense of the true purpose of writing, and further proof that the most reactionary institution in Ireland is neither a political party nor a church, but the public house, in which failure begets failure and erects plinths to the sources of its inspiration.

7 Ignatius Rice

The Christian Brothers have long divided the Irish imagination between those who could see no good in them and those who could see no bad. For those who belong to the highly vocal modern tendency to decry everything about the past, the Brothers signify the tyranny of the dark and forbidding times before enlightenment descended; for those who cling to a nostalgia for bygone times and values, and baulk at the direction of the modern world, the Brothers represent a much maligned past reality with much more going for it than is nowadays acknowledged. Although the 2009 Ryan Report into abuses in Church-run institutions for children came down particularly hard on the Christian Brothers, the truth about them is probably somewhere in between the extremities of remembering.

Yes, it is true that, without the Christian Brothers, many young Irishmen would never have received a proper education, but it would be ridiculous to assert that there is no basis to the association of the Brothers with harsh classroom methods and sometimes with extreme instances of violence and abuse. In times to come, when balance again becomes possible, we shall probably acknowledge that the recent wholesale demonization of the Brothers was something of a distortion. But it would nevertheless be naïve to pretend in the meantime that the picture was as rosy as some of the Brothers' more enthusiastic defenders have continued to aver. Many Irish males who attended any of hundreds of CBS institutions have toe-curling stories to tell of the brutality they suffered at the hands of their teachers. But despite the impression to be gleaned from much media discussion on the subject, such violence was not confined to Christian Brothers-run schools. Corporal punishment was an everyday occurrence in most Irish schools right up to the early 1980s. This culture of violence has many interesting aspects that are nowadays either not understood or misremembered.

For one thing, corporal punishment in schools was widely accepted within Irish society and was indeed regarded as a necessary part of an effective education system. It was not until the 1970s, following a campaign pursued mainly by one man, Dr Cyril Daly, that public opinion began to have second thoughts about the usefulness of beating the lard out of schoolchildren on a daily basis.

The abuses were facilitated and acquiesced in by a State-franchised culture of violence and sadism, sanctioned in the name of education and social control. By the late 1960s, a number of activists were campaigning on the issue, including a group called Reform, founded by a Dublin postman, Frank Crummy. The most courageous and consistently raised voice against this culture was a medical doctor, Cyril Daly, who, in his early thirties in the 1960s, began speaking out against the axis-of-evil comprising the Irish State and the Catholic Church. Dr Daly was, and remains, a practising Catholic who opposed violence against children from – odd as this may have been made to seem – a Christian perspective.

Since Dr Daly's public career ended in the 1980s, with the banning of corporal punishment from Irish schools, his name may be new to most people under forty. But it is largely due to his efforts that Irish children are not today being flogged by thugs calling themselves teachers while the rest of us go about our business.

In November 1967, the *Sunday Independent* published a chillingly realized tableau written by Dr Daly in which he described a 13-stone teacher deploying a carefully stitched leather against a five-stone boy. He observed the attentiveness of the watching classmates, the spoken injunction that the recipient take it 'like a man'. He used the words 'assault' and 'blow'. He described the teacher pausing to say the Angelus before continuing the beating and the forced smile on the boy's lips as he returned to his desk.

In 1969, Dr Daly collected 8,000 signatures for a petition demanding an end to corporal punishment. When he presented the education minister Brian Lenihan with the bound volumes of the petition, the father of the present-day minister for finance asked, 'What do you expect me to do about these?'

There was little evidence of deference about Dr Daly's interventions. He described corporal punishment as a 'scabrous feature' of Irish education and noted that Catholic teachers and prostitutes were the only categories of professional to employ corporal punishment in their work. Dr Daly observed that, although they had been abolished in the army and navy, and not ordered by a court for a quarter of a century, beatings continued to be inflicted on children of five or six. He explained how corporal punishment creates a tension in children that later causes depression and anxiety. He warned that beatings instil a false sense of moral responsibility, centred exclusively on a sense of externally imposed order.

'The Irish child,' declared Cyril Daly in what at the time was a controversial assertion, 'is a human being with human rights.' He appealed to the Church to desist from damaging both itself and the Christian message. He wrote an open letter to the Archbishop of Dublin, accusing the Church and its ministers of a betrayal of trust: 'The Irish child has been dishonoured. He is being given an example in violence. He responds to violence. He respects violence.

Violent men use violence in the Catholic classroom and say this is
the way of Christ. And I say it is blasphemy.'

What jumps out of the archive is how, no matter how irrefutable
the facts, the establishment defended the indefensible to the bitter
end. When Dr Daly denounced the Irish education system on
American television in 1971, he was declared 'anti-clerical' and
accused of letting Ireland down in the eyes of the world. In 1969,
when he spoke at a Labour Party seminar, the event was picketed by
members of the Irish National Teachers' Organisation (INTO)
defending its members' right to beat children. Brian Lenihan said in
the Dáil that corporal punishment should be retained as 'the
ultimate punishment' for children aged eight and upwards. In 1974,
the then education minister Richard Burke described corporal
punishment as 'a necessary sanction to protect the majority of pupils
from an unruly minority'. In one of Dr Daly's surveys canvassing the
views of politicians, a majority ticked the box indicating their
support for abolition, but one politician, surveying the options to
'abolish' or 'retain', crossed out both and inserted 'phase out'. That
politician was Dr Garret FitzGerald.

Given all that is 'known' about the history of violence in the
name of education, it comes as a surprise to many Irish people to
learn that the Christian Brothers were initially set up in opposition
to the culture of violence in Irish schools.

The order was founded in 1802 by a retired businessman,
Edmund Ignatius Rice, whose philosophy of teaching was, in fact,
formulated as a reaction to what he perceived as the excessively
violent nature of education at the time. Rice was profoundly opposed
to the physical punishment of children. 'Unless for some very serious
fault, which rarely occurs,' he wrote in 1810, 'corporal punishment is
not allowed.' The Christian Brothers' *Manual of School Government*,
published in 1832, stressed the effectiveness of 'mildness, affection

and kindness' as pedagogic instruments. 'Blows,' the *Manual* advised, 'are a servile form of punishment and degrade the soul. They ordinarily harden rather than correct . . . and blunt those fine feelings which render a rational creature sensible to shame. If a master be silent, vigilant, even and reserved in his manner and conduct, he need seldom have recourse to this sort of correction.'

In 1825, the British Royal Commission on Education noted of the Christian Brothers-run schools that 'the children are kept in good order and the masters seldom have recourse to corporal punishment'.

The crucial event in the shift away from this enlightened policy appears to have been the Famine of the 1840s. Simply by virtue of the Church's existence and authority in a society with no other indigenous means of self-organization, the responsibility fell to the Church for creating cohesion and providing a moral and social framework to, in effect, ensure that Ireland could contrive to avoid such a calamity in the future.

The radical shift in the culture of the Christian Brothers can be traced to the immediate aftermath of that catastrophe, which followed hard on the death of Ignatius Rice in 1844. By 1851, the Christian Brothers' *Manual* had begun to drop mentions of restrictions on corporal punishment. This trend was consolidated in the 1880s by the passing of the Intermediate Education (Ireland) Bill, which provided for a direct connection between examination results and the payment of funding for schools. In effect, schools were left with a straight choice: adopt tougher teaching methods to compete or risk being passed over in favour of schools with less scrupulous philosophies. Subsequently, the Christian Brothers became markedly more successful, but also more notorious for the brutality of their teaching methods.

8 Ben Dunne Snr

Once upon a time, Irish men dressed in dark suits and white shirts with dark ties. To set off the whole ensemble, they sported black or tan shoes or boots, assiduously polished, and capable of announcing their arrival by the sharp clack they essayed as they walked along. This mode of dress seemed to go well with the demeanour of the grown-up Irish male. He tended not to say much, but nevertheless seemed to be reasonably clear about his purpose in life and what he thought about things. He tended to walk, if not exactly confidently, at least in a way that inspired confidence in the beholder. In short, he looked reasonably dignified and carried himself fairly well.

But forty-odd years ago, all this began to change for the worse. The modern average Irish man, once he has moved beyond the point of thinking about how he looks for reasons related to mating, is now a sorry sight indeed. Nowadays he wears not suits and shirts, but jumpers and slacks in terrible, bland, matching colours, beige and grey, with similarly coloured slip-on shoes made of soft material, which make no sound as he walks. The Irish male may still wear a suit while conducting business, or attending funerals, but he is always a little apologetic about it. He can't wait to get home and change into a cheap tracksuit.

This mode of dress appears to have been accompanied by

something close to an existential shift in the psyche of the average Irish male. Once he tended to move about in public on his own, joining with other males at certain appointed places: the public house, the bookie shop, inside the main door of the church. Now, he tends to go out in public in the company of his wife or girlfriend, who, it is clear, is the architect of his physical appearance. Men have ceased to be men and have become instead mannequins who model not merely clothing but an entire idea of what Irish manhood has become. In this vision of manhood, the male is not an autonomous being but the property of his wife, who disports him for competitive purposes in order to demonstrate (a) his docility and (b) her capacity to control every aspect of his life. In Ireland, we have somehow developed a culture whereby men have come to be regarded, and – worse – regard themselves as the appendages of their female companions. For a man who is in a committed relationship with a woman to indicate independence of mind or dress is culturally interpreted as a sign of actual or potential infidelity.

If you observe such a couple walking into a teashop on a Sunday afternoon, you will, in a single tableau, be able to observe the true nature of sexual politics in modern Ireland. The man, dressed in his beige pullover, fawn slacks and suede shoes, is uncertain of himself, perhaps because he is self-conscious on account of his ridiculous apparel. He glances around uncertainly, as though waiting to be told what to do. He jerks his head tentatively towards a vacant table in the corner, and then to his female companion. She, noting his unspoken proposal, chooses a different table near the door. She indicates her choice by dumping her handbag on one of the chairs and taking off her Prada coat. The man then makes for the counter, looking backwards for signs of what his beloved might desire. You would think that men and women who have been together for anything more than a one-night stand would know one another's preferences in the matter of beverages and muffins, but Irish men in such situations never seem to be confident about doing the right thing and invariably, on reaching the counter, have to go back to consult with their companions in order, perhaps, to avoid a scolding in the end.

Contrast this with the behaviour of, say, Italian couples. On entering the teashop, it is the man who chooses the table, by the simple expedient of sitting down at it. He is dressed in an impeccable blue suit with a white shirt. He is tieless, but only because it is Sunday. His female companion goes to the counter. She knows what he likes and is not afraid of anyone knowing that she is interested in pleasing him.

All this, or most of it, is the fault of one man. His name was Ben Dunne. In 1944, Dunne opened his first department store in Cork. Within twenty years he had become the wealthiest and most influential businessman in Ireland. For Dunne, the customer was king, or, rather, queen. His stores sold cheap clothes bearing the St Bernard label, usually simplified copies of garments produced at much higher prices by the larger international brand names. Dunne was an advocate of 'self selection' retailing: he believed in piling the merchandise on the counter and letting people handle the produce before making a choice.

From modest beginnings Dunnes Stores grew rapidly through the 1950s and 1960s, bringing a semblance of international fashion within the grasp of the ordinary Irish housewife. In 1965, anticipating that shopping was turning into a recreational activity, Ben Dunne opened what would become his company's flagship store at Cornelscourt in south Dublin, Ireland's first drive-in shopping centre. It is said that, after his retirement, he and his wife would drive out there every Sunday to sit outside in the car park and watch the couples coming and going.

Until the arrival of Dunnes Stores, Irish men had tended to buy their own clothes. They went along to the tailor or outfitter, got measured up and went back a couple of weeks later to collect the new suit. But Dunnes changed all that, reducing the average Irish married male to a walking manifestation of his wife's determination to define him.

Dunne, a gruff, conservative man, almost invariably declined requests for media interviews. Once, legend has it, he was approached to appear on the *The Late Late Show*. But when the programme's researcher went to meet him, he answered every question with the Dunnes Stores slogan: 'Dunnes Stores' Better Value Beats Them All.' He assured her that it was his intention to answer each of Mr Byrne's questions in the same way.

Once, back in the 1960s, in an episode that was to have reverberations many years later, Ben Dunne was severely humiliated by one Charles Haughey, then a cabinet minister, who forced him to dismantle a stand he had erected at a trade fair in New York because Haughey felt it was conveying the wrong message about Ireland to the world. On this occasion Ben Dunne was showcasing a new product: the bri-nylon shirt, which could be drip-dried and required no ironing. When Haughey arrived and saw, on the St Bernard stand, a white bri-nylon shirt drip-drying in the air-conditioning, he was, by all accounts, horrified. He approached Dunne. 'What do you think this is?' he demanded, 'the fucking Iveagh Market?' Haughey instructed officials from the Irish trade board to dismantle Dunne's stand.

It was a cruel and humiliating episode for Dunne, but Haughey could do no more than admonish the tide. Perhaps, with his usual perspicacity, Il Duce was able to see the future nadir of Irish manhood, dressed in clothes chosen by women to advertise the reality of the changed relations between Irish men and women in the dawning age of beige.

9 Neil Blaney

Ballymun Flats would become a faithful representation of a people set up by history, a people whose sense of themselves had been interrupted and diverted, a nation in retreat from itself and the stereotypes that had emerged in the national imagination as a result of condescension and interference. It was the product of a people infected by a craven desire to imitate and to conform to an idea of modernity deriving from elsewhere – a model already beginning to be re-evaluated wherever else it had been tried.

From the early 1960s onwards, the national mood became preoccupied by a search for things that would dramatize Ireland's coming-of-age as a re-created society. There was a sense of movement away from the previously held vision of the country in an attempt to escape dark elements of its past. The 1943 St Patrick's Day radio address by Eamon de Valera had acquired in the national imagination a kind of negative motivating stimulus, simultaneously defining what we had been and wished to escape, and unwittingly staking out a new destination. By the early 1960s, fed by the complex interaction of post-colonial uncertainty and desire, it had been decided somewhere deep in the unconscious of the nation that the new destination would be as far in the opposite direction from Dev's vision. Ballymun was to become a totem of this new thinking.

There were to be more ghettoes in Dublin and in other cities, which, back in the 1960s and 1970s, when most of them were created, were likewise intended as declarations that we were moving inexorably away from poverty and darkness. Darndale, Neilstown, Tallaght, South Hill – massive estates on the fringes of our cities – had been intended to showcase the new urban, industrialized Ireland, to bear witness to the extent to which we were becoming 'like other modern societies'. Conceived to a blue-print based on Hollywood B-movie notions of what modern living should be like, they were designed for the future blue-collar generations that would man the factories of the new country. Within a few years they had become like the dirt under the carpet of a new fangled, spick-and-span Ireland lacking any sense of its own intrinsic absurdity.

Ballymun was, among such estates, a unique folly, an icon of the failed project of modernization, a symbol of the depth and density of official incoherence, the Mother of all Ghettoes. The seven fifteen-storey, low-density tower blocks were to be Ireland's first high-rise apartment blocks. One of the core absurdities of Ballymun was that its high-rise element was utterly, insanely superfluous, given that the towers and flat complexes ate up enough ground to house an equivalent number of people in conventional estates. Ballymun was created as an urban utopia by a generation in exile from its roots in the land. The fact that, being constructed around the time of the fiftieth anniversary of the 1916 Rising, the seven towers were each given the name of a different revolutionary leader, was merely the tin-hat on this living, ironic representation of the pathology of post-colonial confusion. Ballymun captured our helpless predilection for imitation in the form of an ironic monument to those who had died for what they hoped would be a complete and complex form of independence.

Here, as a monument to our incoherence, were our seven Towers of Babel in the heart of a wasteland of imitation.

When the 3,000-unit Ballymun project went to tender in 1964, the government specification required it to be constructed 'as speedily as possible, consistent with a high standard of layout, design and construction and to acceptable costs'. The towers and other apartment complexes were constructed from prefabricated concrete panels cast in an on-site factory. Demand was brisk and prospective residents were subjected to assiduous interview. Problems soon began to manifest themselves, however, with poor maintenance leading to perennial tenant disgruntlement. The inefficient heating system, which could be regulated only by the opening of windows, was a prime focus of complaints, being both costly and inefficient, with poor insulation causing severe heat-loss though the walls of the towers. The lifts were another source of ongoing grievance. The cumulative effect of these difficulties was the phenomenon of transient occupancy, which nurtured instability and fed an emerging drug culture.

Many of the people who ended up in Ballymun were only one or two generations removed from the land. In this, yes, reservation, a new type of Irish person emerged – urban but without strong urban roots, Irish but disconnected from the essentially natural identity of Ireland. It was as though these people had been put out there while we waited for modernity to take. The dominant motif was of a taming of the wilderness, combined with the imposition of something unmistakably alien that, in a country endowed with both space and beauty, could have arisen only from some deep sense of self-doubt and hatred of our natural inheritance.

Ballymun will forever be associated with the then Fianna Fáil Minister for Local Government, Neil Blaney, from Donegal, and mythology had it that the towers had been strategically placed so that politicians, with a wave of the hand in the back of the state car, could indicate them to visiting dignitaries on the way in from the airport.

But as the Lemass boom of the early 1970s rapidly dissolved into a reprise of pessimism that persisted into the 1990s, unemployment and the absence of even the most basic infrastructure ensured that this intended showcase of modern living turned into a nightmare ghetto, with none of the advantages and all the disadvantages of urban living.

Ballymun came to function as a cautionary example of something to be regarded as an unavoidable element of state-driven social intervention. In the final decades of the twentieth century, it became useful for journalists as a source for illustrations of poverty with its pram-pushing teenage girls or freckled boys on horseback. But somehow these never led anywhere, as though the existence of such places was something unavoidable and perhaps even remained, in some backhanded way, a tribute to the modernity of Irish society.

It may seem unfair to place all the blame for this on the shoulders of one man, but had the project been a success, Neil Blaney would have basked in any glory that might have arisen. He must therefore be conferred, if only symbolically, with the blame. The ultimate irony is that Blaney was one of the most unapologetic republicans to emerge in Irish politics in the second half of the twentieth century.

10 Gay Byrne

When, at the end of the twentieth century, Gay Byrne retired as host of *The Late Late Show*, his departure was attended by a predictable avalanche of commentary focused on his contribution to the 'modernization' of Irish society. Reading account after account of how Gay Byrne had led Ireland out of the depths of Stygian blackness, it was difficult to keep stifling the yawns. For anyone reading such treatises would have been driven to the conclusion that, were it not for Gaybo and his *Late Late*, the people of Ireland would have been incapable of boiling an egg or operating a flush toilet. And not merely was *The Late Late* essential to our ability to stand unaided on our hind legs, but it was always unmissable.

In fact, *The Late Late* was never any good except when you didn't see it. You could sit week after week watching a monotonous parade of mediocrities and then, Lent over and your penance completed, the one week you skipped out to the pub you could be sure that nobody would talk about anything else except what had happened on *The Late Late*. This suggested that either you were unlucky to always go out on the wrong nights, or *The Late Late* was never as scintillating in reality as was subsequently 'remembered'. It was afterwards, in the days following certain shows, rather than on the screen on Saturday or, later, Friday night, that the legend was created.

Of course, in the beginning nobody expected *The Late Late* to be anything other than a mildly diverting talk show. Its 'importance' was not an issue until the 1980s, when it was adapted as part of the apparatus of modernization employed to propel us forward from the ignorance of pre-television Ireland. It then became the main springboard used to catapult us out of a mythical and distorted version of our past, which had been caricatured to provide the maximum quality of propulsion. Since reality was much more complex than this caricature required, it was necessary for those who sought to bring about certain changes in Irish society to manipulate the evidence so as to increase our desire to 'progress' by making the past seem as revolting as possible.

It is even taken half seriously by some people, that, as the Fine Gael TD Oliver J. Flanagan once jokingly put it in a Dail speech, 'there was no sex in Ireland until Teilifis Eireann went on the air'. In truth, there was far more sex in Ireland before *The Late Late*, if only because people had nothing else to do in the long evenings. Declining fertility rates in recent decades suggest that people started having less sex from about the time *The Late Late Show* went on the air.

A researcher on *The Late Late* once related how, when he compiled a selection of the programme's greatest hits for some anniversary or other, he was afterwards assailed by people wondering why he had not included the episode known as 'The Bishop and the Nightie'. He asked them if they knew precisely what this item entailed, and they responded with claims that this was one of the seminal moments in Irish television history. Yes, he said, but do you know that in the episode of 'The Bishop and the Nightie' there was no bishop and no nightie?

All that occurred on the screen on the night in February 1966, when this stirring tale of modern Ireland unfolded, was that a woman, taking part in a light-hearted party game based on a format 'borrowed' from another TV station, when asked what colour nightie she had been wearing on the night of her honeymoon, replied 'none', before quickly adding 'white'.

It can hardly have been news, even in the most 'traditional' parts of Ireland, in 1966, that people sometimes took their clothes off before going to bed together, but this did not prevent the Bishop of Clonfert from immediately contacting the Sunday newspapers to inform them that he would be preaching a sermon in Loughrea on the following day in which he would denounce *The Late Late Show* as immoral and request his flock not to watch it again. The newspapers insisted on presenting the issue as a major moral confrontation, and the story was a front-page lead on Sunday and Monday. On the night of the programme, only three people rang the station to complain about the broadcast, and two of these were exercised because the idea had been ripped off from another TV network. Thus, only one person in the country felt sufficiently morally outraged by the item to pick up a telephone and complain, and this person was the secretary of the Bishop of Clonfert. Only through the intervention of the media did the event become one of the groundbreaking episodes in the creation of modern Ireland. Something banal would be said on the show, and some publicity-hungry cleric or county councillor would make it into a federal issue. A 'national debate' would ensue about the decline in moral values or some such nonsense. This suited the agenda of the modernizers because the impression was thus given that they were hard at work confronting the dark forces, when in reality nobody but a handful of lunatics was in the slightest bit bothered. *The Late Late* did not, as is suggested, 'open up' Irish society; what it 'opened up', more often than not, were the ample mouths of some of the more ridiculous of our public figures. If we are to judge from what we 'remember' about it, the alleged 'influence' of *The Late Late Show* was all over and done with within five years of first going on air.

Indeed, 'The Bishop and the Nightie' affair was regarded as such a seminal feature of Ireland's socio-sexual development that, in the late 1970s, when RTE was spring-cleaning its vaults, that particular programme, along with virtually all other *Late Late*s over the previous two decades, was wiped. It is probably just as well for those seeking to elevate the importance of Gaybo and his show that nothing of these supposedly earth-shaking episodes is preserved: if it was, we would today be able to perceive their utter tedium and banality.

So, when we talk about the importance of Gay Byrne's contribution to Irish society, we should be a little more specific. The change was not so much in the reality of Ireland as in the public perception of it. The change was that we began to say what was going on, in public, on live television, rather than simply thinking it or muttering about it among ourselves. The change was in the nature of talk, rather than in the nature of events. Those who celebrate the influence of *The Late Late* are celebrating themselves and the success of their particular agenda.

And, yet, nobody could look back at the vast span of Gay Byrne's broadcasting career and declare him an uncritical proponent of modernization in the crude sense that some of his eulogizers have implied. Gay Byrne was and is a complicated man, a broadcaster who was driven first of all by the desire to make interesting radio and television programmes. He did not, as is now suggested, set out to manipulate the material of a society in flux in order to bring about change more rapidly than would otherwise have occurred. He would also be the first to propose that some of the 'opening up' he is credited with facilitating has had as many baneful consequences as beneficial ones.

11 Pope John Paul II

The marking of the anniversary, in September 2009, of the 1979 visit of Pope John Paul II to Ireland comprised part nostalgia and part self-satisfaction, the nostalgia being less for the Pope than for the feeling of innocence which had come to be associated with those times. The analysis went something like this: the Pope, personable but representing an outmoded form of thinking, came to Ireland at approximately the moment when we began to wake up and smell the cappuccino. After the Pope left, the Church fell apart, and Irish society 'matured' into new understandings.

The numbers who turned out to see the Pope were remembered thirty years later as evidence of the vigour of Irish Catholicism at the time. It was, we were repeatedly told, the end of an era, or as one dissident priest crudely put it, 'the last sting of a dying wasp'. Conventional wisdom assumes that Irish Catholicism remained vibrant until the emergence of the clerical scandals of the 1990s, starting with Bishop Eamonn Casey (one of the stars of the papal visit) and his American squeeze, and then continuing in a way that very rapidly cast Casey's adventuring in an increasingly benign light.

There is another way of looking at it: that really the papal visit was simply a splurge of sentimentalism, empty of any real engagement with the mission of this rather remarkable Pope, or even any understanding of what he stood for. A deeper assessment also suggests that the later public scandals became pretexts for the many who were already failing to find an engagement with Catholicism to declare publicly their alienation. It was far easier to 'explain' your disillusionment by reference to a betrayal than to look deeper into the condition and ask questions that might indicate a more complex picture.

The real problem, prevailing long before the arrival of John Paul II, related to the reduction, over the previous century or so, of Christianity as expressed in Irish Catholicism into two thin strands: moralizing and emotionalism. The Church had become a moral police force, and Christ, seeming incompatible with this function, had been externalized and suffused in an aura of sentimentality. Christianity had become separated from reality, except in so far as reality consisted of rules and rituals. Strangely, the mass media persona of John Paul II seems, oddly, to have embodied both the characteristics of these two strands infecting the Irish Church. This was nothing like the full truth of John Paul, but mass communications are poorly adapted for complex truth-telling. By turns, the Pope came across as avuncular and finger-wagging, smiling and stern, doctrinaire and affectionate, and in doing so dramatized precisely the condition of the culture he was addressing. He had to his personality three distinct elements: the charismatic 'pop star'; the philosopher poet and the stern bearer of simple injunctions. But he also gave rise to a certain 'à la carte' tendency in his audience, which warmly embraced his personality while overlooking his message and remaining deeply ignorant of its roots in reason and human experience.

Nothing about his Irish visit managed to transcend the dualisms provoked by his public personality. In his various homilies that weekend in September, the Pope talked about peace, family values, the law of God. But, for all the positive emotionalism unleashed by his persona, his language served mainly to underline the emerging sense that Christianity was unlikely to be in harmony with the coming times. The words the Pope used were designed to shore up something that really no longer existed, if it ever had. For all his brilliance, John Paul was slightly behind what, deeper down the culture was trying to comprehend. John Paul II is remembered with the deepest affection in Ireland, even by some who otherwise have nothing good to say for Catholicism. But it is largely his charisma that is remembered, rather than his more enduring qualities: his understanding of human nature, his clarity of moral vision and his insistent repudiation of utopianism.

An unfavourable comparison is often made in Irish conversation between Benedict XVI and the man who preceded him. This is almost entirely spurious. Few who praise John Paul and seek to bury Benedict as 'reactionary', 'right-wing', 'dogmatic', could name a single point of theological or philosophical difference between them. Of the two, Pope Benedict is by far the more tuned-in to the condition of modern culture. He has a profound grasp of what has happened to Christian societies, including Ireland, beset by a shrivelling of reality through ideology and language. What is called secularism, operating in a pincer movement with the reduction of Christianity to morals and sentiment, has removed from our cultures the means for a human being to access in reality a total definition of himself. Modern man remains secure only for as long as he can remain within his own constructs, but even a glance out the window, at the horizon of knowable reality, casts him into a dizzying terror. His only hope lies in distraction: money, intoxicants, false ideas of freedom and cultures renovated to minimize the human exposure to the Absolute. This is the secret history of the Celtic Tiger and a condensed explanation for the rage and grief that has followed it.

John Paul, of course, recognized these conditions too, and diagnosed them in his writings. But in his more generalized public utterances he tended to offer a simplified solution: a return to lost values and humbler aspirations. His public patronized him and cheered him, but remained certain that he was a kind old man whose ideas had passed their sell-by date.

A few years after the visit of Pope John Paul II, Ireland was briefly convulsed by a summer-long spate of quasi-religious phenomena in which, all around the country, public statues of Christian icons – in particular at shrines to the Blessed Virgin dating from the Marian Year of three decades previously – were said to have moved and danced and shimmied. For months on end, the nation seemed to speak of little else, as new reports came through on almost a daily basis. Even convinced atheists went along and said that they had seen the statues move. Undoubtedly this odd phenomenon spoke of something deep in the heart or soul of the Irish people, perhaps by way of articulating a feeling that could not be spoken otherwise: that despite the surface shift towards what has been acclaimed as an increasingly 'rational' worldview, the desires of the human heart continue to seek a correspondence for themselves. A quarter-century and another recession later, these questions are more 'live' than ever.

12 Charles J. Haughey

There is a phrase from Ben Dunne's testimony to the Dunne Payment Tribunal that goes some way to explaining the scale of the cultural phenomenon that once was Charles J. Haughey. Dunne, son of the eponymous founder of Dunnes Stores, told the tribunal about his understanding that there had been a plan by those seeking to raise money on Mr Haughey's behalf to approach a number of businessmen with a view to obtaining donations of perhaps £150,000 from each. Mr Dunne said that, when approached, he volunteered to meet the target of £1 million in full. He recalled for the benefit of the tribunal his reactions at the time: 'I think Haughey is making a mistake trying to get six or seven people together. Christ picked twelve apostles and one of them crucified him.'

That a leading businessman should in 1997 make a connection between a top politician and the Son of God would in practically any other country be enough to discredit his testimony as the ramblings of a lunatic. But in Ireland the reference resonated something in the cultural perception of Charles Haughey in a way that made it slightly less than ridiculous.

Irish politicians have not until recently been mere human beings. They were, in the past, Gods, Devils, Chieftains, Popes and Anti-Christs. This condition of political quasi-superhumanness

was one of the things the modernizing forces sought to erase, and was the main reason why Charles Haughey came so often into their sights. That battle was played out in issues like the North, the economy or the liberal agenda, but the succinct truth is that Haughey became the most controversial figure in twentieth-century Irish politics because he alone on the Irish political landscape played to the old culture. He was the last great tribal chieftain of a people being dragged into what was tendentiously termed 'the modern world'. Nobody was as adept at playing off the two worlds, at tapping into the sensibilities of both. Charles Haughey lived and ruled through an era when old values were being dissolved and turned into money. Bereft of a personal vision, he tried to simulate the appearance of a visionary by aping ancient values and their adherents, even while he was up to his oxters in the green slime of the material world. He used money to create the illusion of magic.

Like the fat chieftain whose reputation for qualities of leadership rests on the irrefutable evidence that he is able to feed himself and will therefore be able to feed his tribe, Haughey played to the deep insecurities of his post-colonial people by suggesting that what he could do on his own behalf, he could do on theirs. We looked at his (metaphorical) ample belly and felt reassured. This was the 'secret' of Charles Haughey's political success: because he was rich, we imagined, sneakily and at the back of our minds, he could make the rest of us rich as well.

He delivered, too – up to a point. If our previous financial embarrassment bore a passing resemblance to Mr de Valera's notions of frugal comfort, our subsequent Celtic Tiger-period shut-your-face-and-take-a-look-at-my-wad style of prosperity was undoubtedly closer to Charles Haughey's brass-necked approach to the management of money.

When Haughey walked into Government Buildings in February 1987, Ireland was on the verge of bankruptcy. A decade later, the Irish economy was the envy of Europe. It scarcely needs pointing out that this turnaround in the national fortunes had far more in common with the manner of Charles Haughey's own enrichment than with the careful, muddling husbandry of his political rivals.

Charles Haughey did to the public finances in office – particularly from 1987 to 1992 – what the McCracken Tribunal would reveal he had been doing to his private finances for several decades. Consider the following key elements of the strategy employed:

(1) Borrowing: The strange thing is that Mr Haughey was a late and reluctant convert to adapting this particular methodology to the running of the national economy. In 1974 he warned that 'We should be very conscious however of the fact that we must not come to accept budgets which are, as a matter of course, going to finish up with a deficit which has to be borrowed.' It was actually his great arch-rival, Dr Garret FitzGerald, who first promoted the idea of national borrowing on a grand scale. In 1966, a deficit/GNP ratio of nearly 1 per cent was regarded as a serious crisis; eleven years later, the ratio was roughly ten times that figure and Dr FitzGerald was fretting publicly that we might not be borrowing enough. Following that infamous January 1980 TV appearance, in which he lectured the public about living beyond its means, Mr Haughey took a leaf out of his rival's book and settled into running the country along much the same lines as he ran his personal finances: borrowing from Peter to pay back Paul.

(2) Begging: On reclaiming office in 1987, Haughey found his borrowing options considerably circumscribed and diverted his energies to adapting his private talents for begging to the global economic arena. In consequence, in each year of the 1990s, Ireland

Inc. received transfers from the European Union amounting to an average of 7 per cent of GDP.

(3) Inducements: During this period also, foreign industrialists and bankers were offered irresistible inducements to locate here rather than someplace else. Thus was Ireland Inc. transformed into a money-laundering operation for multinational capital.

It's a most peculiar thing that, even in the prosperous Tiger years, we seemed only too delighted to accept the benefits of Mr Haughey's philosophy and efforts in the public sphere, and yet excoriated him for the time he spent perfecting the arts of begging, borrowing and stroking in private before he came to be in a position to exercise these talents in our interests.

There was always a sense of the miracle of the loaves and fishes about Haughey's wealth and status. The baskets flowed over and gave no sign of being diminished by extravagant consumption. For many years, when confronted with the implausibility of his material circumstances, he would bluff, stonewall, make jokes and quote Shakespeare. This created a sense that he was either totally clean or utterly impervious to detection. If you were to ask some of his most steadfast supporters whether they would have preferred their leader to be honest or invincible, they would have said that they would prefer him to be invincible. That he for so long gave the impression of such imperviousness suggested itself also as a form of magic.

But magic, in a modern society, is no match for the law, or for the rational gaze of the determined modernizer. In the end, the Last Fat Chieftain was finally exposed, not by a Judas but by a disciple named Ben who feared the duplicity of others and thus led his hero into the final, fatal trap. The mystery was solved. The source of Haughey's wealth was sordid and pitiful. There had been nothing magical about it.

And this, indeed, was the source of the greatest disappointment with the Fat Chieftain: the discovery that he accumulated his own riches not by wizardry but by supplicating.

His unmasking as a clumsy conjurer was merely a prequel to the exposure of a far greater illusion: the Celtic Tiger, which he had tweaked into being with his sleights-of-hand. And this in turn rendered us even more disappointed – not just with Haughey, but more fundamentally with the very idea of our becoming wealthy. Perhaps our first instincts had been right: we were not cut out for this sordid business of acquisition. And perhaps this is why there is no hope now, for the very name of Haughey reminds us of that shameful time when we were naïve enough to believe in magic.

13 Garret FitzGerald

In a 2010 speech criticizing the Taoiseach Brian Cowen in the wake of what he called a 'botched' reshuffle, the Fine Gael front bench upstart Leo Varadkar chose as an unfavourable comparison not one of Cowen's Fianna Fáil predecessors, but the man who had been a legend in his own party. Cowen, having doubled the national debt, he said, was not a Lemass or a Lynch, but a Garret FitzGerald. Varadkar went on to predict that the Taoiseach would end up writing 'boring articles for the *Irish Times*'.

The outrage that followed was of an ecumenical nature. Members of every political party, and none, sprang to the defence of the now octogenarian former Taoiseach. Varadkar came under pressure to apologize, but seemed to hold his nerve. He later announced that he had written to FitzGerald 'explaining' his remarks. As likely as not, there was some petty personal reason for Varadkar's tirade. But, still, the very passion of the response he provoked seemed to speak as much about the truth of his observations as anything else.

FitzGerald is a deeply admired figure in Irish society. Indeed, he has come to be loved and respected by almost everyone, not least because of his extraordinary energy, humility and approachability since leaving office. He continues writing his weekly *Irish Times* column, which, contrary to Varadkar's assertion, is not always boring. (Although once, the same copy was inadvertently published two weeks running and not a single reader contacted the newspaper to complain.) He is a regular guest on radio and television panels discussing politics and economics. Often, nearing the end of a seminar on some vital public matter, when the time comes for questions from the floor, Garret stands up and delivers himself of a detailed analysis of the merits and shortcomings of everything that has been said. Sometimes, strangers gaze at him in wonder and declare: 'That guy is fantastic! He should go into politics!'

Garret FitzGerald was for nearly five years, between 1982 and 1987, the leader of the Irish government, and in that time, as Leo Varadkar said, he doubled the national debt. But nobody really blames Garret for that. It was really all Charlie Haughey's fault. If Haughey had kept his promises, Garret wouldn't have inherited such a disaster of an economy to begin with. In the 1980s, there was only one game in town, and that was the drama of Garret the Good versus Charlie the Great National Bastard. It is possible to state this in a way that seems ironic, even sarcastic, at Garret's expense, but the fact of the matter was that, of the two men, FitzGerald was by far the more likeable and the more morally upright.

But he was also a disastrous politician. He spoke constantly of why he had 'come into politics'. In fact, he spoke constantly, period. He talked and talked until the donkeys of Ireland were entirely bereft of hind legs. Garret is a deeply intelligent and interesting man. He reads voraciously: history, economics, theology, philosophy, poetry. He is truly brilliant. He likes listening to classical music. He loves his wife and children. Coming to power at a period when, for the first time in nearly 150 years, a generation of young people was able to think about staying in Ireland, he attracted the hopes of both the young people and their parents, thus ensuring that Fine Gael gained, under his leadership, the highest number of seats in its history. Since his departure as leader, the party has come nowhere close to a similar achievement.

U2 singer Bono was among those who became briefly infatuated with Garret, whom he invited down to a recording session in Windmill Lane. In return, Garret appointed him to a body set up to look at issues affecting 'the youth'. Bono, realizing the whole thing was just a talking shop, slipped away after the first meeting.

On the face of it, Garret seemed to be the perfect leader for a new country coming out of the mists of a blighted history. He had charisma, intellect and boundless energy. He had been a working journalist, so he understood how the media worked. He surrounded himself with savvy advisers, who understood things like image and communication strategy. He had vision – he wanted to usher in a non-sectarian, pluralist Ireland as a way of reassuring unionists across the border that Rome no longer ruled the roost. He had courage: he was not, generally speaking, afraid of bishops. He attracted women and young people into Fine Gael. But there was something missing, and this something missing became the tragedy not just for Garret but for all those who placed their hopes at his door. He was absent-minded, but that wasn't it. His absent-mindedness simply added to his professorial persona – like the way he emerged one day in public wearing unmatched shoes. He explained that he had put them on in the dark because he hadn't wanted to wake his wife by putting on the light. It was all so Garret.

He talked and talked. Cabinet meetings went on interminably as he argued and debated with himself. One colleague at the cabinet table at that time was quoted thusly: 'He has an extraordinary mind, but it has no filter, no perspective, no defence mechanism against all the interesting but irrelevant details which come to distract him.' He had an obsession – no, a love affair – with figures. It was he, really, more than anyone, who identified the scale of the problem with the Irish economy in the early 1980s. But he was unable to do anything about it except make it far, far worse.

When, as a guest on the Terry Wogan show on BBC television as his administration shuddered towards its apocalyptic conclusion, the Limerick-born host asked him if things at home were not truly abysmal. Garret grinned and said that, in fact, Ireland was now producing more computer scientists per capita than the United States. At the time it was seen as evidence of how out of touch Garret was, but within a decade, with the economy back in the black and Ireland rapidly revealing itself as the IT hub of Europe, Garret's professorial pronouncement didn't seem quite so nutty.

In the long run, of course, it didn't matter. With the benefit of hindsight, the difficulties of the 1980s were a minor blip compared to what happened in 2009. But the real problem about the Garret experience was that it would be a long time again before the Irish electorate would be able to trust the type of educated, sophisticated man who read books, listened to Mozart and would, later, write for the *Irish Times*. We became wary of talkers and thinkers, which is why, perhaps, we ended up with monosyllabic mediocrities and affable actors who never, ever get their shoes mixed up.

14 Bishop Eamonn Casey

Nearly two decades on, Bishop Eamonn Casey's 'sins', or at least the ones he was punished for, suggest themselves as the flaws of a good man. He had knocked up an American woman, Annie Murphy, who had given birth in 1974 to a boy called Peter. All things considered, he was a high-class kind of sinner.

In May 1992, when Peter Murphy was seventeen, it all started to spill out. The *Irish Times* had been sitting on the story for weeks and eventually went with a partial version of it, mainly an element relating to Casey's payment of some £70,000, said to have come from a diocesan account, to Annie Murphy's 'partner' as a 'settlement for Peter'. A couple of days previously, Casey had mysteriously resigned as Bishop of Galway, after the *Irish Times* made contact with him concerning the information it had gathered. Gradually it emerged: Annie Murphy had been the daughter of an American friend of Casey's, who had come to Ireland on the run from a broken marriage, and had become 'involved' with Casey, who had been Bishop of Kerry at the time.

The Irish people were stunned, and not purely because it was impossible to come to terms with the idea of a bishop having sex. Casey had been no ordinary kind of bishop. In an era of clerical austerity, he had been a breath of fresh air. Roly-poly of both body and spirit, with his mellifluous Kerry accent he caused people to

smile when he started to speak. He was known to like big cars and
to drive them fast, and to 'enjoy a glass of wine with his meals'. He
would go on *The Late Late Show* and sing 'If You're Irish, Come
into the Parlour' and tell jokes and talk and talk until the cows came
home. Gaybo would be rolling around the floor.

If he had not been wearing the purple rig-out, you would never
have known Casey was a bishop at all. And yet, he was one of the
most attractive figures in a Church that seemed to have forgotten
about the necessity to convince people that religion was not entirely
an occasion of misery. Casey had been one of the stars of the visit
to Ireland of Pope John Paul II in 1979. He also seemed to do much
more than other bishops of the kind of things Christians were
supposed to be doing: helping starving Africans and suchlike. As
Director of the Catholic Housing Aid Society, he had been
responsible for establishing sixty-five branches in the UK, enabling
thousands of homeless people to find places to live. As Bishop of
Kerry he had taken a special interest in developing services for
young people. As chairman of the Catholic Third Word Aid
organization Trócaire, he was a constant campaigner on issues
affecting the poorest people on earth, frequently excoriating
politicians for their failures. He had also been a vocal critic of the
Reagan administration's record in Central America.

For many years, the Irish people had studied Bishop Casey and
wondered what he was so happy about, and now they knew. And,
although the idea of a bishop having sex was unthinkable, in
another sense it fitted perfectly with the undertow of Casey's
character. In one way, it caused people a great deal of existential
relief to realize that there had been a perfectly reasonable
explanation for Casey's apparent perpetual good humour. And it
also offered people the prospect of relief from their own sins. The
idea that a senior bishop had succumbed to the temptation of an

American divorcée was something that, deep down, people wanted to celebrate rather than condemn. But this was not a culturally approved response, either in the old world of the Catholic Church or the 'new' one led by the *Irish Times*, so they had to keep it to themselves. Many people grinned inwardly when they thought of Casey and wondered how many other adventures he might have had, but outwardly had to join in the general clamour of cant and humbug in a society only too delighted at this opportunity to prosecute such a monumental example of a senior cleric being caught out doing one thing while preaching another. So, whether because of the woman, the baby, the money or all the above, Casey had to go.

As the years unfolded and the floodgates opened up on revelations of clerical sexual abuse and cover-up, Casey gradually came to look as if he'd been hard done by. What, after all, was Irish society trying to say? That it did not approve of bishops having sex? On the contrary, there began to be a growing demand for married priests, women priests, men and women priest who were married to each other, transvestite priests, transsexual priests and so forth.

What was it? That Irish society could not tolerate bishops having sex while seeming to oppose such activity for others? That it was really, as the *Irish Times* tried to pretend, about the money? Or, as some of the more pious critics insisted: that the worst thing was Casey's refusal to leave his position and marry Annie Murphy, or his failure subsequently to develop a relationship with his son. Perhaps, indeed, this latter was Casey's only real offence, added to Murphy's claims that he had initially tried to persuade her to give their child up for adoption.

When you rinse it all down, it seems Casey had to go because he had behaved hypocritically. In truth, of course, there is not necessarily always something morally decisive about believing and stating one thing and, in certain circumstances, doing another. On the contrary, the Catholic Church insists that we are all sinners but that sins may be wiped away in the sacrament of confession. Perhaps unsurprisingly, the heavily secularized mass culture of modern Ireland, which calls for more and greater sexual freedoms, is far less forgiving than the tyrant bishops, when it happens to be a bishop who is caught with his trousers down.

Mercy and compassion towards Casey appears to have been the unspoken wish of the Irish people. Casey himself later claimed that he had received 1,500 letters and that only two were critical of him. Why could Eamonn Casey not simply have confessed his sins, conducted his penance in private and got on with his work? Would this not have been the best way of demonstrating how Christianity was supposed to work? In due course, he could have gone on *The Late Late* and confessed his sins to secular Ireland. God knows, in the years that followed, we could have done with a bishop who could come on television and sing 'The Foggy Dew' and tell a yarn or two about what the actress said to the bishop to cause him to fall out of bed.

15 Albert Reynolds

Albert Reynolds, who, when asked during the 1992 general election campaign about claims that he and the leader of Fianna Fáil's coalition partners, Desmond O'Malley, never spoke outside the cabinet room, responded that this rumour was 'crap, pure crap'. There followed a tsunami of sanctimony and high dudgeon, as opponents and journalists, supposedly offended by Albert's language, spun into verbal tizzies at the offence and drama of it all.

The then government Press Secretary, Seán 'Diggy' Duignan, later recalled in his book *One Spin on the Merry-Go-Round* that this episode genuinely damaged Reynolds. It probably did, but only because a couple of people in the media just wouldn't let it go. It was an issue of taste, we were told, of how the Taoiseach was expected to comport himself, of the coarsening of public life, the dragging down of high office and the end of life as we knew it.

If you tell people often enough that something is important, they start to believe you. But really this was the seizing by opportunistic actors of a chance to put flesh on an existing prejudice. Albert had never been popular outside his own party supporters, and was deeply loathed by many media people.

Reynolds, unlike Bertie Ahern, had a proven record as a businessman, having made his fortune in the dancehall boom of the 1960s, later moving on to the dog food business. He had started out as a lowly clerical officer with CIE, the state transport company and, when working as a clerk in Dromod railway station in the late 1960s, was noted for the way he would get all his work done in the morning and spend the rest of the day looking after his growing dancehall business. With his brother Jim, he built and operated more than a dozen dancehalls, using the profits from one hall to build another, borrowing judiciously and expanding exponentially, always dealing in cash. One time, when Albert was involved in a car smash on the way home from a dance, the road was littered with the night's takings, which he had casually stowed in the boot. This back-story in the dancehall business was the source of much ignorant commentary by journalists who, by sheer force of repetition, created the impression that the showband boom had been some kind of reactionary ideological movement rather than an opportunity for people to make money by enabling other people to have fun. But, having laid their groundwork of prejudice by associating the Taoiseach with the 'Country 'n' Western Alliance', the new 'evidence' was easy to work into the thesis that Reynolds was an uncouth redneck unsuited to high office.

Although the story of Albert's ultimate demise is complex, there is no doubt that the 'crap' episode contributed to the drip-drip of prejudice which, in the end, rendered him a pushover for the Salomés who came looking for his head.

When Albert was elected Fianna Fáil leader and Taoiseach, he set himself to cleaning up the party after CJH, or at least seemed keen about being seen to do this. The appointment of his cabinet amounted to an outright purge of Haughey loyalists, which resulted in deep resentments being carried into the long grass. When you are at the mercy of the delicate arithmetic of a coalition arrangement, it is not a good idea to open cracks in your own parliamentary party.

Albert was eventually undone as the result of a trumped-up crisis about an alleged attempt to suppress an extradition warrant for the paedophile priest, Father Brendan Smyth. From the instant when the political crisis began to unravel in mid-November 1994, the media seemed resolved to prosecute the issue to the death. The allegation was made that, owing to outside interference, a warrant from Northern Ireland for the extradition of Smyth had been inordinately delayed at the Attorney General's office. The Democratic Left TD Pat Rabbitte stood up in Dáil Éireann and announced that he was aware of a document that would rock the State to its foundations. There was a letter in existence, he insisted, from a senior cleric, requesting the Attorney General not to proceed with the Smyth warrant. The Labour Party, Fianna Fáil's junior partner in coalition, demanded a head – Reynolds's or his AG's – or they would pull out of government. The controversy was further muddied by allegations that Reynolds had misled the Dáil in relation to another case involving a paedophile priest, which became infamous as 'the Duggan case'.

A Dáil committee, set up in the wake of the affair in an attempt to establish whether there had been any wrongdoing associated with the delayed warrant, found no evidence of outside interference with the AG's office. There had been no involvement by the Catholic Church. The matter of Reynolds's alleged misleading of the Dáil emerged as being the consequence of nothing more sinister than chaos. No letter had been sent by any cleric to any politician. The foundations of the State remained unrocked. It was all crap, pure crap. But by then it was too late: Reynolds had resigned and, in the shemozzle that followed, a change of government had occurred, with the Labour Party shifting beds to join a rainbow coalition with Fine Gael and Democratic Left.

In due course it became clear that the Reynolds government had been brought down by a series of misunderstandings arising from an opportunistic campaign by a nest of unelected advisers, and that this campaign was driven by a media vendetta in pursuit less of facts than of the scalps of various people associated with Fianna Fáil.

Reynolds was a smart businessman and an exceptional politician. He played a key role in establishing the groundwork for the settlement of the Northern conflict and presided over a key period in the stabilization of the Irish economy following the disastrous 1980s. But he provoked in a new breed of commentator and politician an almost visceral dislike, based on snobbery and ignorance of the reality of the Irish personality and the complex nature of the journey we had made from poverty to prosperity.

Had he not thrown in the towel, he might well have led the country for another decade, applying his usual horse sense to national affairs. It is inconceivable that a man of such common-sensical outlook on reality would have presided, as his successor Bertie Ahern did, over the descent into madness that supplanted Irish economic policy in the early years of the third millennium.

Perhaps the greatest tragedy of the past two decades has been the fact that, beset by pseudo-bohemian snobbery and small-town prejudice, Albert Reynolds threw in the towel and walked away.

The long and the short of it, as Albert himself might put it, is that he was forced out on the basis of allegations that subsequently failed to stack up. Had he stood his ground and allowed the Labour Party to walk, he might have saved his leadership and his government – and ultimately, perhaps, saved his country from the ruin that would begin to engulf it about a decade later.

16 Shane MacGowan

Perhaps nobody, in all the history of traffic between the two islands controversially known as 'the British Isles', has done as much to make the native Irish feel inadequate as a shambling songster called Shane MacGowan. With his band, The Pogues, MacGowan, a young London-Irishman claiming connections to County Tipperary, did something with Irish music that was unforgivable.

In fairness, MacGowan did his best to camouflage himself in a way that would undersell his arrival, and avoid provoking the congenital ire and resentment of the native. His gap-toothed grin and incoherent speech patterns seemed designed to counterbalance his capacity to hear Irish music as it had never been heard before and to render it anew for a generation of Irish people who immediately began to kick themselves in the realization that they should have been able to do this for themselves. Were it not for his unprepossessing appearance and self-effacing mode of non-musical communication, MacGowan might well have provoked homicidal fits of jealousy among the indigenous population.

For when an intelligent and unprejudiced Irishman heard The Pogues, he was immediately struck by a sense of inadequacy that made him want to cry. (Strangely, women did not seem to feel the same thing, perhaps because they felt less of a responsibility to

define, by Joyce's stern injunction, the uncreated conscience of their race.)

The music of The Pogues was in one sense pure formula: traditional Irish ballads put through the punk mangler, a straight-forward forced collision of incongruous elements. Perhaps an uninitiated ear might hear the music and not be moved by anything other than a deep existential laughter, an urge to dance, or just to jump up and down. But this was a luxury unavailable to the Irish, for we knew what this was. It was our culture as it might have been if it hadn't been interrupted. It was something from the parallel zone of Irish possibility, something that seemed blissfully to be unaware of how history had actually happened and was proceeding on the basis of this glorious ignorance.

MacGowan, from a slight distance, had been able to hear and identify something in the music from which we had grown up trying to escape – a tradition that we, the insiders, could approach only with great caution, because it attracted and repelled us in almost equal measure. The preciousness and exaggerated reverence with which the native music of Ireland had come to be regarded by those seeking to effect a reconsecration of indigenous virtue had provoked in the young an uneasy scepticism that, by its very nature, made them feel both guilty and free. Surrounded by the mythic balladry of their fathers, the post-Emergency Irish had rushed headlong into the arms of David Bowie and Johnny Rotten, pausing only to barf discreetly on account of a rumbling distaste for what had been emerging as an 'authentic' musical version of the native soul. The mawkish, sickly-sweet balladry of the be-sweatered jolly Paddies and the puritanical purism of the custodians of the indigenous 'tradition' were the inevitable consequence of the execution of Pearse, the unavoidable pay-off from the insularism of Rev. R.S. Devane.

In a healthy society, any undue solemnity towards the artefacts and baggage of the past is, as appropriate, lightly or roundly mocked by the young. This challenge is what keeps a culture honest. But in a society in which the question of culture fore-shadows matters of life and death, the necessary contempt of the young is suppressed out of a fear of causing undue offence. In Ireland, unable to square the circle, we of the liberated young of late twentieth-century Ireland found new outlets of self-exploration, shaking off the sentimental yoke of a culture that reduced everything to victimhood. But still we could not entirely walk away.

Our attitudes and policies towards the ballad revolution of the 1960s had been characterized by both an involuntary affection and a distaste born of the grim passion it invoked among our elders. It touched on something at once laughable and sacred. Our rebellion against its earnestness was countered by an involuntary awe at its indisputable if tattered dignity. This stuff, we knew, had been road-tested under conditions of great privation and desperation, and it still travelled with a lifted heart and a grin of something not too far off exultation.

But this also troubled us. The pain in the music could not help coming to the surface, sometimes in the form of a sentimentality that seemed to ooze like an inadequate self-understanding struggling to find the right key. It disturbed us, and yet we could not bring ourselves to mock it. There was something here that reminded us of something, even if we could not bear to listen long enough to work out what it might be. This music, perhaps more than anything else in the culture we had inherited, provoked in us a capacity for self-recognition that the culture we now inhabited, though ostensibly of our own creation, or at least of our co-option, did not enable us to approach. We possessed neither enough love nor enough hatred to do with the music what The Pogues did. But, the moment we heard it, we knew what it was. The last thing any of us had imagined was that the leaden, desperate ejaculations of our drunken uncles might be turned into gold.

For here was a music that simultaneously expressed both our attachment to a slightly false version of ourselves and an ironic repugnance of it. As though insisting on some undefined ethic of rigour and clarity, it reached into the heart of the music, wrenched the sentimentalist heart out of it and cast it away. It was at once a celebration and a refusal, a kick and a kiss. It was a soundtrack for the neurosis born of the post-independence failure of Irish culture to find a way of jump-starting itself – but also, for the same reasons, a living, leaping, soaring blurt of the spirit that had become suppressed. It was a deconstruction of something recognizable as having been put together in slightly the wrong way – the clue that much more than this was fundamentally wrong. The Pogues offered a rejection, but only of the superficial presentation, the sugar coating. The deeper qualities were subjected to a firm and passionate embrace, pulled together and kicked onstage. The music conveyed an unmistakable sense of nostalgia, but also a rage that seemed to announce itself as deriving from the overall tragedy of Irish history. There was mockery, too, but of a gentle kind that seemed to comprehend the extent of the pathos to be dealt with. It had both pride and the awareness of a received loathing. It celebrated and mocked at the same time. It did not choose between allegiance and disdain, but crammed them both into the same mix.

Shane MacGowan, by virtue of both his intimacy with and 'outsiderness' in Ireland, had access to the culture of his ancestors but was not hidebound by the characteristics which caused the natives to become struck down by cultural paralysis. Removed by a generation and a stretch of water, The Pogues had been enabled to achieve a degree of detachment which gave them a vantage point on

Irish culture that the insiders could not achieve. This slight distance from the clammy embrace of the culture allowed them to understand something that baffled the indigenous population. On hearing the results, we were jerked into a new sense of ourselves, but also visited by new feelings of inadequacy. How had we missed this? What else were we missing? And who was this bastard MacGowan to be showing us up in this way?

17 John McGahern

'Real life,' John McGahern once observed, 'is too thin to be art.' He was talking about the necessity to reimagine reality before it can be turned into fiction. His novels contained elements of autobiography, but they were not autobiographical. Yet, his final book, written at the very end of his life, was his own autobiography, *Memoir*. Among its many interesting insights is the confirmation it provides of what had previously been a woolly impression concerning the extent of McGahern's reworking of the detail of his own life into his stories.

It could plausibly be argued that *Memoir* was McGahern's single literary mistake. By chronicling the literal reality from which he had forged so much of his fiction, it exposes the undercarriage of his imagination to a scrutiny that may ultimately risk damage to his reputation in the eyes of future generations unencumbered by the present-day deference to certain artists by virtue of the scale of their reputations. Before the publication of *Memoir*, McGahern's other books had a total life of their own, set free from literal connections by the nature of the fictional contract. After *Memoir*, they become something else – not fact, but no longer quite fiction either. By setting down the raw material from which his essential life-perspectives were forged, McGahern left a hostage to fortune: an apparently faithful record of factual events for literary critics and academics to pore over.

Because of the deference problem, it has not been remarked upon that there is something extremely odd about *Memoir*. Although dominated by McGahern's memories of his parents – the mother who died when he was a child and the father with whom he carried on a disturbed relationship into adulthood – *Memoir* has a feeling of being artistically incomplete. Several times in the book McGahern states that he never understood his father, Frank McGahern, a Garda sergeant cast as a brooding, violent presence in the lives of his wife and children. Actually, it's clear that the young McGahern disliked, perhaps even hated, his father, and that this dislike or hatred was not in any degree dissipated by the writing of *Memoir*. There is no moment of grace between father and son that might be deemed the cathartic moment of the book. At no point does the author seem to reflect on this in a detached manner. It is as though he is utterly unaware of it.

There are many ethical issues arising from the modern fad for biography-as-art. The fashioning of literal literature out of the raw reality of real human lives, especially of those – generally males – who become so blackened in the reporting as to leave in the world only a negative impression – is a deeply dubious phenomenon. The modern view is that anyone has a right to tell his own story: the truth must out, and let the consequences take care of themselves. This is 'art', after all.

But there is also a question of justice. Usually it is the case that individuals damaged by such literatures are, by virtue of being deceased, in no position to rebut any of the charges. No human being can claim to have a monopoly on the truth about another. But no human being exists only in the perspective of another. Even when relationships are fraught, there are always two sides to the story. It is a heavy responsibility, then, when a writer decides to put on record what may turn out to be the sole account of the existence of another – named – human being.

John McGahern's reputation as one of the English language's greatest novelists is well deserved. He is correctly regarded as a giant of fiction writing, an astute observer of the subtext and nuance of human communication, with a poet's eye for the human dilemma at the point of contact with reality. But the artist has a duty to tear his vision from the prism of a culture and see clearly into the lies a society may be insisting upon telling for all kinds of warped reasons. *Memoir* raises the awkward possibility that, in certain respects, John McGahern was unable to do this.

Since the aftermath of the Famines of the 1840s, Irish society has been run by the diktats of an ideology that elevated the mother to the status of put-upon Madonna, and reduced the father to that of brooding menace on the periphery of family life. This crude act of social engineering was effected by the Catholic Church, for the purpose of controlling the somewhat licentious appetites of the Irish and preventing a repetition of the calamity that their libertine habits had caused to befall them. After independence, this initiative gained a new impetus. In a society that had been traumatized twice – by famine and by civil war – the Church usurped the power of the civil authority and assumed, in effect, the role of moral government, recruiting the mother in the home as its agent of control, and with her assistance reducing the father to a barely tolerated provider devoid of moral authority. This resulted in a crude caricature of masculinity that became normalized in Irish society to the point of invisibility: the silent, passive-aggressive father and the saintly, martyred mother. Adding outrage to injury, having banished the father to the fields or the fair, the culture then laughably interpreted the rage born of his marginalization as the roar of the oppressor.

Such stereotypes abound in the work of John McGahern – for example Mahoney in *The Dark* and Moran in *Amongst Women* – seething, pent-up beasts whose emotional retardation is rarely examined but merely exists, like the hawthorns or the meadow blowing in the breeze. In their own way, then, these stories add to the accumulation of prejudice concerning the psychology of the Irish male: creating a further sense that silence or violence are his primary modes of expression.

This stereotype has been deeply damaging in Irish culture, and continues to have baneful consequences for men in a society that, despite being 50 per cent male, appears to have no capacity to articulate the reality of male experience.

To be fair, McGahern would have been the first to repudiate the idea that he had a role as a social historian. He once told the *Guardian* that he was suspicious of all ideologies: 'Joyce called them those big words which make us unhappy. I think they have very little to do with life and everything to do with the struggle for power.'

Yes, but this surely places an added burden on the artist to be alert to the way ideologies can infect reality and inflict great pain on human beings. To simply say that one is not interested in ideology is to say that life can somehow remain immune to its effects. This is a cop-out greatly favoured by artists and writers in today's Ireland.

The reception of *Memoir* was universally and unambiguously glowing, and to a considerable extent deservedly. But it was striking that these reviews, and indeed virtually all the commentary that has attended McGahern's life and work, appeared oblivious of the extent to which the writer had harmonized with the discordances of a deeply damaged culture. In the wake of his death in 2006 there was, for example, much of the usual guff about McGahern's depiction of the 'patriarchal reality of Irish society'. By this analysis,

Moran in *Amongst Women* (seemingly more than loosely based on McGahern's father) is the tyrant king who rules over all within his gaze. Just as it is clear from *Memoir* that McGahern had little interest in the roots or nature of his father's demons, so also is it obvious that in his writing of fiction he accepted at face value many of the flimsiest myths of his society. But, caught between the hyper-visible power of the Church and the invisible power of an undeclared matriarchy, Moran's rage was really the rage of the impotent.

Memoir suggests that the explanation for McGahern's myopia was that he himself had not yet begun to see into the total truth of his own father. Whether he should have written the book or not is beside the point: more interesting is what all this tells us about how a culture manages to recruit the wounded among its spokespersons to preserve a convenient version of itself long after this has become outdated or even irrelevant. Writers, who should be challenging and dissenting, very often contribute to the malign weave of a culture by virtue of a failure properly to interrogate their own experiences and backstories. For who, if not the artist, will describe things other than as they seem?

18 Mike Murphy

There has been a tendency, since the meltdown of the Irish economy in mid-2008, to look backwards for reference points to the 1980s. Some commentators have been trying to depict the 1980s as a dark and forbidding landscape, much in the way that, a generation ago, people tried to present the 1950s as having happened in black-and-white. This is bad history and completely unfair to a time when, by virtue of innocence, lack of expectation and long familiarity with hardship, the effects of financial privation were not accorded the repetitive, gnawing emphasis they are today.

Although things were certainly bad back then, there was not the constant sense of foreboding there has been this time around. Most people recognized that the breadth of human life embraces more than economics. There was a general sense that not only would Ireland survive the recession, but that the future was broadly promising. People got on with things, often against odds that would nowadays cause people to lie down on the roadside and die.

Among the reasons for this underlying sense of relative positivity was that there wasn't this constant commentary, from early morning until midnight, telling us how awful everything was. Back in the 1980s, it was possible to get up in the morning and go about your business with the radio on, without constantly being impelled to slit your wrists. In those days, Radio One opened up with a music and chat programme, presented by Mike Murphy, which ran until ten, interrupted at eight and nine by news bulletins and *It Says in the Papers*.

Mike had the ability to give you a sense of heroism about being up and about in the morning. He had a comedy slot called 'yowza yowza' and he bantered between the farming news and the weather (there were no traffic problems in those days), and played shite music, which is what everyone expected first thing in the morning.

After the nine o'clock news, he did a long interview until ten, often with a well-known personality or public figure. This was usually interesting, and deeply serious, because Murphy was interested in people and how they ticked, and unafraid of getting into what people thought and felt about life in general. Then we had the *Gay Byrne Hour*, which was occasionally as good as it was later 'remembered', and after that John Bowman presented *Day by Day*, bringing all the current affairs stories that nowadays we get assaulted with on *Morning Ireland* before we can even get out of bed. It was a matter of tone and perspective; the whole morning package seeming to be rooted in a more balanced perception of reality. There was less depression then, far fewer suicides and no phone-ins.

There are a good few people who could be blamed for what has happened to the Irish sense of perspective, but the most obvious is Mike Murphy. He was still a relatively young man in the early 1990s when he turned his back on broadcasting and went off to get rich for himself in property development. Had he not done so, it is likely that the current disposition of the Irish people would be a great deal sunnier than it is.

Murphy was an exotic character. There was a story going around at one time that he had failed his Leaving Cert. This was untrue. Mike had never taken the Leaving Cert – it was the Inter he failed.

Also a failed actor, he became one of Ireland's most successful broadcasters in an era when there was some serious competition. He didn't seem to have an obvious talent, except, perhaps, the ability to make fun of his lack of obvious talents, but somehow the sum of his incompetence added up to something uniquely wonderful. He could make people laugh without being offensive. And yet, when the occasion demanded it, he could address himself to serious matters. He was the ideal man to wake you up in the morning, because he refused to get too heavy about anything until he was satisfied that his listeners were wide awake. Then he introduced his daily guest – perhaps a politician, artist, writer, or environmentalist. Once the people of Ireland had had their porridge, Mike seemed to think, they were ready for anything.

But then Mike fecked it all there and fecked off for himself. The people of Ireland were left to the tender mercies of David Hanly and David Davin-Power, saying 'Good Morning' in unison, like the Two Ronnies, in a way that put your teeth on edge. The jokes in the morning became fewer and farther between. Mike moved to lunch-time, but eventually threw his hat at it altogether.

Nobody could quite believe that Mike was serious about jacking it all in. It was true that he had not been regarded as quite the equal of Gaybo, but he had his own following and was as loved by the public as it is possible to be. But Mike was adamant and never once looked back.

There is an episode that some observers believe was a key factor in his decision to quit. In the spring of 1985, an article appeared in *Magill* magazine that caused many people to gasp in horror. It was written by somebody called Donal Whelan, and it was a vicious article about Mike. It praised Mike's radio programme and sense of humour, but complained that, latterly, something had been happening to Mike. He had, said Mr Whelan, 'discovered art'. Mr

Whelan berated and jeered at Mike for his new-found interest in art, which it was alleged had brought about the destruction of a glorious career. Mike, he felt, had become pretentious and had lost his chirpiness. 'The man who knew no fear,' wrote Mr Whelan, 'the broadcaster as happy as the day is long, who joked and jeered until the cows came home, has been looking at paintings and reading books. When he sits in the studio he carries the burden of these things with him. He wants to be serious and enlightening and it is awful to watch him try.'

It was a cruel and nasty article, but it was also, in a certain two-dimensional sense, accurate. It seemed to foretell, by looking deeply into the core of the problem with Mike Murphy, a tragedy that would soon befall the entire nation: we would all succumb to seriousness and ponderousness.

Nobody had ever heard of 'Donal Whelan' before. A few people who used to hang around the pubs on Merrion Row, close to where the *Magill* offices were situated in Dublin, were aware that 'Donal' was actually a well-known journalist with aspirations to becoming a novelist. They also noted that, when Mike Murphy started to present an evening arts progamme, 'Donal' became a regular panelist and was getting along famously with Mike.

It was only a matter of time. Someone told Mike who Donal was. One evening in the foyer of the Abbey Theatre, Mike approached this aspiring novelist and berated him loudly for his cowardice and duplicity. It was, by all accounts, savage.

Perhaps it was this episode that caused Mike finally to abandon his duty to keep the Irish people in a good mood. Years later, when the aspiring novelist had become a very great novelist indeed, and someone made a passing reference to the episode, Mike wrote a letter to the *Irish Times* saying that he was reading the latest novel by the artist formerly known as Donal Whelan and was enjoying it hugely. But this made the Irish people even sadder than before, because it merely confirmed the extent of their loss. They had always known that Mike Murphy was a good egg, but now their grief knew no bounds. Mike had forgiven Donal Whelan but he still wasn't coming back.

19 Conor Cruise O'Brien

It is not necessary to have agreed with Conor Cruise O'Brien about everything – or even about anything – to be able to recognize his importance in Irish life and culture. In our time his name has become a byword for a certain deeply unyielding mindset in relation to the so-called Irish Question. Perhaps because his view of Irish history was inordinately skewed by a desire to effect changes in the present, the Cruiser seemed to believe that the past could be re-entered and altered almost in the manner of a Harry Potter storyline. From the 1970s, he became the High Priest of revisionists who set out to deconstruct the alleged myths of Irish nationalism so as to pursue a reconciliation with unionism. Many Irish people, though agreeing that the Provos were an abomination, never came to accept that in order to isolate armed republicanism, it was necessary for southern Irish society to distance itself from all sense of moral grievance concerning its own history. When the revisionist blueprint extended to excoriations of the 1916 leadership and calls to downplay the gravity of the Great Famine, many found themselves having to excuse themselves from the anti-Provo express.

While many nationalists in the Republic agreed that the Provos had been able to take advantage of a legitimate historical grievance to justify acts of the most appalling barbarism, they had difficulty

with the idea of dismantling their entire sense of history. Many supporters-in-principle of Cruise O'Brien's position, while recognizing that there was a paradoxical validity to the idea that a change of heart among nationalists offered the best, perhaps the only, possibility of forward movement, would have liked him to at least hint that his motivation was pragmatism rather than principle.

There are those who say that the Cruiser, by his promotion of censorship measures that for years kept the 'men of violence' off the airwaves, did much to prolong the 'Troubles' by contributing to the isolationism of the republican movement and precluding an open public discussion that might have served to end the conflict sooner. This is an unknowable quantity now, although the degree of progress achieved after the dismantling of censorship in the 1990s suggests that the gagging of the gunmen might have been a mistake.

There are those, too, who hold the diametrically opposite view: that only because of the Cruiser's insistent repudiation of armed republicanism, and the logic of censorship that emanated from it, did southern society become 'honest' enough to edge towards an accommodation with the other tradition. It may not be an exaggeration to say that, without Dr Cruise O'Brien's moral leadership, we would never have achieved the resolution of the Good Friday Agreement.

Wars are not fought solely by men bearing guns. Behind the troops in the trench or the sniper in the undergrowth is the moral authority supplied by the unwritten mandate of the many who tacitly support the cause being pursued through violence. Wars cannot last long without such energy behind them. It follows, therefore, that settlements do not come about merely by negotiation between the active combatants, but also through a process in the hearts and minds of those who supply the active combatants with the moral authority to carry on the war. This suggests a cultural problem, which can be dealt with only by a delicate snipping of the atavistic wires that carry the signals and impulses that, down the line, lead to bombs going off in the street.

In this process there was a need for a special kind of leadership, from people with a special capacity for collective empathy with their own tribe. There has always been a great deal of pious nodding towards the Cruiser's intellectual capacities, and undoubtedly he was one smart cookie. But really he was a type of tribal shaman, who depended as much on instinct as on reason of the conventional kind. During the years of conflict, he turned his own name into a byword for something that really did not emanate from him at all, but was rather an element of the culture he belonged to. Because of his enormous gifts of understanding, he has tuned into a strain of our collective emotional life and gave it words.

As a writer, he engaged deeply with the issues he wrote about. His 1972 book, *States of Ireland*, remains one of the most compelling and elegant chronicles of the roots of Irish tribal conflict. Even if you disagree with its conclusions, it is impossible to be unaffected by the quality of the writing.

States of Ireland had been written, he stressed, from the Catholic, 'specifically Southern Catholic', side of the fence. He had tried to understand some of the feelings shared by most Ulster Protestants and to communicate some notion of these feelings to Catholics in the Republic. As a result, he had been 'accused of being hypersensitive about the Protestants, and caring little about the Catholics'. In fact, he insisted, the reverse accusation would be more true. 'It is to the Catholic community that I belong. This is my "little platoon", to love which, according to Edmund Burke (whose family were in that same platoon), "is the first, the germ, as it were, of publick affections". I am motivated by affection for that platoon, identification with it, and fear that it may destroy itself, including me, through infatuation with its own mythology.'

It is interesting to note how this passage is dominated by the concepts of 'feeling' and 'affection', rather than by intellectual or conceptual thought. With this book, Dr Cruise O'Brien was attempting the expression of something deep within the soul of his own people. We can choose to describe this as the self-hating neurosis arising from the colonial experience, or as the voice of our collective conscience, awakening to the new responsibilities of a post-victimhood Ireland. Perhaps it does not matter how we describe these feelings, so long as we recognize their existence. For this clarity about ourselves, we owe Conor Cruise O'Brien a significant debt.

But there is another side. Few objective observers could have disagreed with the Cruiser's description of the Provos as 'haters'. But he seemed to forget that there was hatred also on the other side, that hatred begets hatred and that, in the end, it can be difficult to tell the angels from the devils for all the hate clogging up the system. Perhaps his point was that it was not our responsibility to critique the other side. But from the nationalist viewpoint, it some-times looked as though he'd simply changed tribes.

Perhaps his greatest flaw was that he was unable to see other than the dark side of his own people, and this, tragically, caused him to become an undeservedly marginalized figure. His pessimism affected his judgement and led him eventually to a profound error about the chances of reconciliation. In an address delivered at Queen's University Belfast in 1978, he said that the reason many people could not see that Irish nationalism and unionism were incapable of reconciliation was because this idea was 'so desolatingly devoid of all comfort'. We all, he said, 'find it hard to accept bad news even when it is true'. For many years he predicted an outright descent into civil war, and, even after the settlement of 1998, continued to preach gloomily about the prospects of a lasting peace. His apocalyptic predictions have been shown to be largely mistaken. The truth may, however, be more complex: perhaps even his overstatements contributed to the eventual outcome.

But perhaps, too, he had become so certain that collective ambivalence was the problem with Irish history that he refused to adjust his opinions in a changing landscape. Having convinced himself and others that the problem in the North was a particular interpretation of the nationalist narrative, he became focussed on pursuing and permanently imposing this argument, rather than looking squarely at the prevailing conditions. The ultimate tragedy, for him and Ireland, was that his pessimism resonated too harmoniously with the despair of his times, opening up the appalling possibility that, in spite of the moral integrity of his leadership, his main influence was to delay the peace for a generation.

20 Frank McDonald

There is a possibly apocryphal story about a stranger who goes into a West of Ireland bar and, spying a man in the corner in a state of some melancholia, clearly determined upon drinking himself to death, asks of the barman what the matter is with this troubled soul. The barman explains that the man is a carpenter by trade and, once upon a time, was the area's foremost expert in the construction of stairs. No matter how awkward the job, how confined the quarters, how complicated the configuration, he was called in to advise and implement. He was The Man Who Could Figure Out Stairs. 'What happened to him at all?' the stranger enquires. 'Some bastard,' replies the barman, 'invented bungalows.'

One could be forgiven for thinking that many of those who commentate upon the nature of housing and planning in today's Ireland are secretly related to this unfortunate individual, such is the zeal with which they have taken to condemning the bungalow and all who reside in it. For twenty-five years, until the very recent past, the public conversation seemed to take it for granted that the most significant planning problem facing Irish society was something called 'bungalow blight' or 'one-off housing', a phenomenon not entirely unique to Ireland but somehow seeming to provoke here a uniquely sanctimonious response. Hardly a week seemed to pass without some architect or planner making an intervention in which the phenomenon of one-off housing was designated the most serious crisis facing the Irish environment, or calling for a commission to be appointed to investigate rural housing. In one such *Irish Times* article, 'How We Wrecked Rural Ireland', one former planner lamented the 'nests of bungalows' which he complained were to be found 'all over the place'. He lambasted Irish people for their lack of appreciation of 'urban values' which, he said, might have served to convince people that more beautiful houses could be built in towns and villages. He described bungalows as 'uniformly awful' and condemned the trend whereby farmers were able to sell off land as sites, allowing outsiders to come into an area and build more bungalows. He called for a prohibition on the sub-division of family farms for this purpose.

This nonsense all began in the 1980s with a series of articles written in the *Irish Times* by that newspaper's otherwise excellent environmental correspondent, Frank McDonald. It was Frank who coined the term 'bungalow blight', a play on the title of a book of simple house designs, *Bungalow Bliss*, which he blamed for the spread of one-off housing in rural areas. He characterized the development as a cancer infecting every part of the country. 'Throughout the length and breath of the country,' he wrote, 'rural areas are being destroyed relentlessly by this structural litter on the landscape – litter than can never be removed. And this cancer is so pervasive that for every private house built on a suburban housing estate, at least one other house is built in the middle of the countryside.

'If this was Eamon de Valera's dream of a country "bright with cosy homesteads", it has turned into a nightmare. Because what is happening, in effect, is that we are abandoning our towns and villages in favour of colonizing the countryside.'

Frank cited some statistics that, he said, illustrated the 'frightening' spread of this bungalow 'blight'. These indicated that the output of one-off houses in rural areas had doubled, from 5,530 to 11,050, between 1976 and 1983, and was now accounting for more than 53 per cent of all newly built private houses, compared to just 35 per cent ten years before. In County Monaghan, he claimed, one-offs accounted for a 'staggering' 80 per cent of all private house completions.

Frank also bemoaned the fact that much of this housing seemed to be 'urban-generated' – built for people with no functional connection with agriculture. 'Most of them work in the nearest city or town, but they choose to live in a rural environment for status reasons or because they simply like the fresh air. In short, they are in the countryside, but not of the countryside. The doctor, the solicitor, even the butcher and the dancehall owner, used to be quite happy with homes in town; now they have fantasies about Southfork-style ranch-houses. Indeed, one of the phenomena of modern Ireland is the proliferation of vast mansions faking *Dallas* or *Dynasty* on the outskirts of so many provincial towns – the palazzi gombeeni, as one Dublin architect has scathingly described them.'

Stirring stuff, but actually a load of horlicks. The most graphic communication in this particular article was of the arched conde-scension with which Dublin architects are wont to regard their fellow citizens. The tragedy is that such a fine journalist should join forces with such prigs against the citizens of a free republic, enabling the discussion about housing and planning policy to become monopolized by self-important Dublin 4 architects who imagined the countryside existing so that they might occasionally drive across it in their big cars. McDonald's campaign sparked a one-sided, undemocratic debate, conducted on the basis of metro-politan bias, spurious aesthetics, snobbery, dinner party politics and a fundamental lack of perspective on the nature of Irish life. Thanks to the Bungalow Blight campaign, the very idea of a self-standing house in the countryside came to be associated with backwardness, sleveenism and poor taste꞊ Oil.

In fact, the figures quoted by Frank McDonald indicate that the increase in one-off housing was occurring within a sustainable model of development based on real human need. In the West of Ireland, certainly, the alleged 'rural housing sprawl' that developed from the 1970s onwards, was at last a hopeful sign that the region's long history of decline and depopulation might be over. People were taking up opportunities to build houses in locations to which they had some family or emotional connection. For the most part, there was little or no speculative dimension, Ireland continued to have one of the lowest levels of population density in Europe, and what was wrong with people preferring the fresh air?

Thus, a tiny elite of interested individuals, with agendas ranging from snobbery to social engineering, managed, by pooling their ambitions and influence, to create an unaccountable and largely invisible nucleus of official prejudice against something as completely harmless as a self-standing house in the countryside.

Meanwhile, but by no means unconnectedly, the real cancer in the Irish planning process went unremarked upon until it was too late.

By the middle of 2008, when the Irish economy finally went into meltdown mode, it began to be clear that the greatest problem facing the Irish planning environment was not one-off housing after all, but, lo and behold, the numbers of houses which had been built in towns and villages, usually as a result of tax incentives, for which there was no prospect of finding buyers or occupiers. Most of these developments had been favoured by planning authorities because of an ideological view that clusters of houses in towns and villages were a vast improvement on one-off housing. With the increasingly prohibitive nature of the planning climate, which in some areas gravitated towards an outright ban on one-off rural housing, people who would once have routinely obtained permission to build homes on their family farms, had ceased to bother asking. Instead, the focus shifted to developers who sought to promote housing schemes within towns and villages, and it was largely from this shift that the crisis developed.

By 2010 it had become clear that the crystallization of the Irish economic disaster was to be located and observed in the phenomenon known as 'ghost estates'. These were the unoccupied developments that now studded the landscape, usually attached like haemorrhoids to villages and small towns, amounting to some 300,000 housing units that could neither be sold nor rented. Gradually it became clear that the only solution to this problem was to raze all such developments to the ground.

Frank McDonanld cannot be blamed for this situation. Nevertheless, it was what often seemed to be his relentless campaigning on one-off housing that led to the emergence of a culture of unreason in Irish planning circles, and this made the eventual catastrophe inevitable. If, instead of pursuing the ideological path laid down by McDonald, the Irish planning sector had pursued a policy of encouraging one-off housing, it is likely that much of this disaster might have been averted. The Dublin architectural community has been silent on this point.

21 Desmond O'Malley

In July 1989, following the successful coalition negotiations between the Progressive Democrats and Fianna Fáil, Desmond O'Malley got to his feet in Dáil Éireann and said: 'I want to acknowledge the courage and skill exhibited, particularly by Deputy Haughey in recent weeks, courage and skill which I know he possesses in abundance, and which has been utilized in the national interest during this time.' Once again, in adhering to the national interest, Mr O'Malley had managed to emerge with the outcome most congenial to himself. This man, who had once characterized Mr Haughey as unfit to hold power, was now suggesting that it was in accordance with the public interest that Mr Haughey hold the second highest office in the land.

A number of people with long memories had the bad manners to remind Mr O'Malley of his previous emphatic position concerning Mr Haughey, articulated most memorably in the wake of his own expulsion from Fianna Fáil in 1985, when he said that Haughey's role in the Arms Crisis of 1970 had rendered him unfit for positions of public power. Now, the Irish people could only gasp in admiration at how O'Malley and his Progressive Democrat colleagues were prepared to grub around the place in their ministerial cars, their bottoms shifting uneasily on the compromising upholstery, because the national interest required them to humble themselves in this disagreeable way.

Back in 1985, when O'Malley founded the PDs, there had been much talk about the imminent realignment of Irish politics into a more orderly, 'European', configuration. It would be only a matter of a short time, we were assured, before the tribal divisions of Irish politics began to divide coherently into left- and right-wing elements, as had happened everywhere else.

This was the PD pretext, or part of it. Another significant element was ethical, or at least nominally so. The PDs were to be the 'party of integrity', in contradistinction to Fianna Fáil, the party led by the great PD nemesis. Only when Charles Haughey was buried at a crossroads with a stake through his heart, it was said, could the PDs be wound up. And so, eventually, it would come to pass, with the PDs surviving Haughey by just a couple of years.

No matter how they tried to dress it up, Haughey was the sole reason for the existence of the PDs. Haughey attracted a deep-set loathing among the emerging elites of the new Ireland who mistrusted the swash of his buckle and despised the hair on his *nouveau riche* head. Haughey's arrogance, pride, pretensions, rudeness, sulphuric aura and, above all, formidable political ability, created tremors across a whole swathe of the modern Irish mind. The PDs eventually became the personification of this resentment, which has retrospectively claimed justification on the basis of what the McCracken and Moriarty tribunals managed to dig out – but they had nothing to go on in the beginning except envy and spite.

Everything else was pretext, elaborate self-justification to camouflage the banding together of individuals and cultural interests with no grander purpose than the defeat and destruction of a pretender so exceptional that his existence assured all mediocrities with pretensions and ambitions that they had been born at the wrong time. In a sense, the PDs began not in 1985, but at the moment, some two decades before, when certain members of an

aspirant political generation took one look at the swarthily prepos-
terous figure of Charles J. Haughey and realized they were going
nowhere while this guy remained on the pitch. The unfolding story
of Irish politics in the coming half-century was defined by this
encounter, which shaped the evolution of Haughey's own
personality as much as it shaped the reaction to him.

When Desmond O'Malley first entered the Dáil in 1968, on the
sudden death of his legendary uncle, Donogh, Charles Haughey
had already presided, as Minister for Finance, over one economic
boom. Two decades later, he was as Taoiseach to pave the way for
a second. In between, he spent most of his time and energy fighting
for his political life, as the pygmies around sought to dispatch him
to the political locker room. When you filter out the moralistic
soundtrack, these are the important features of the Irish political
topography of the past half-century.

There are two kinds of iconoclast: the kind who wants to tear
down the establishment because of pure idealism and the kind who
threatens to pull down the establishment so the establishment will
move over and invite him to join it. Des O'Malley, as evidenced by
his subsequent willingness to get into bed with his nemesis (in 'the
national interest' or otherwise), was the latter kind.

He was, to begin with, an unlikely politician, and especially an
unlikely Fianna Fáil politician. At college he had been a bit of a
leftie, and, despite his later nodding towards the right, this seems to
have fitted his personality better than anything he subsequently
tried. At one time he was a traditionalist fulminating against forni-
cation and Anglo-American culture, and then was reborn as the
defender of authentic republican values. He was comfortable in
the role of minister, of apparatchik, of ideologue, but never as
politician. He was dogged but uncharismatic. He was unprepossessing of appearance and brittle of manner. His voice grated on

your nerves. The terrible truth, however, was that, no matter what he claimed to stand for, Dessie just looked plain wrong. Once, in an effort at a makeover, he emerged with a new haircut. Everyone gasped. Some observers laughed out loud. But in no time at all, everything came to naught. All the king's hairdressers were unable to stop that demon tuft of hair on the back of his head from sticking up like Liberty Hall no matter what they did.

Similar conditions of philosophical incoherence and flawed aesthetic seemed to dog the party he founded. No matter what the PDs tried, it all came to very little, because really there was nothing much behind the party but ambition and resentment. Of the twenty-three-year history of the PDs, nearly fifteen were spent in government with Fianna Fáil, the party they set out to destroy. This relationship both enabled the PDs to exist long after they might otherwise have become irrelevant and also, paradoxically, killed them off with the kind of kindness that Fianna Fáil and man-eating cobras do well.

The type of voter who voted PD was fickle and self-interested, the antithesis of the FF mujahideen. By getting into bed with the enemy, the PDs cut off their own lifeline, believing that their achievements while in office would speak for themselves. They were too arrogant to anticipate that Fianna Fáil would steal their clothes and suck their veins dry, adapting anything remotely usable among their ideas to the culture that FF understands as no PD could ever do.

Although Desmond O'Malley struck many poses on different issues in his long career at the top of Irish politics, he seemed always to be more concerned about sounding principled than in actually achieving anything that might genuinely be for the good of the country. Even his principled image was mainly for effect.

In 1986, shortly after he founded the PDs, he and his party

colleague, Bobby Molloy announced that they were giving up their ministerial pensions because there was 'no moral justification' for still-serving politicians receiving such payments. Less than a decade later, both men began accepting their pensions again, and Dessie explained that it was because they had got 'no thanks' for their earlier gesture. Gone was the question of moral justification. Gone were the values. Gone was the national interest. All that remained was the pragmatism of a man whose view of morality related purely to the behaviour of others.

The lesson of the final demise of the PDs was that Irish politics has never been, and never will be, ideological. There has not emerged, and will never emerge, a left–right divide. Fianna Fáil has always known this, and in the end the PDs came to know it too. Their sole enduring contribution to Irish politics was the imposition of a form of priggishness in the public arena that causes principle to read instantly as hypocrisy. They were the Pharisees to the tax-collectors of Fianna Fáil, the stern federal marshal riding shotgun on the James Gang.

22 Big Tom

If music is prophetic – as Jacques Attali persuasively argued – then the mood of present-day Ireland was best anticipated not by the nation's ancient tradition of folk music, nor by the folk boom of the 1960s, and not even by the latter-day rock giants like Sinéad O'Connor and U2, but by the maudlin, self-pitying oeuvre of Big Tom and the Mainliners. The connection, of course, is not so much with the content of lost lovers and dead mothers, as the tone depicting what was approximately an emotion: a deeply, inconsolably felt condition of self-pity, expressed in the most direct and inarticulate way.

What is absent today is irony, a quality of 'Country 'n' Irish' that most people – not excluding Big Tom himself – seemed to miss. And yet, in the 1960s and 1970s, Big Tom unselfconsciously brought irony to parts of Ireland that other purveyors of cultural content could not reach. Until his audience dwindled away around the end of the 1980s, he enabled a whole generation of youngsters to see the same thing simultaneously in two different ways. This was partly because of an unacknowledged cultural divide between town and country, and partly because of the absence of choice for young people in those days. At least half of Big Tom's audience comprised the newly minted pop kids of post-Lemass Ireland, who had grown up listening to Radio Luxembourg and John Peel. Very often, the 'country' showband was the only show in town, so if you wanted to go out, that's where you had to go.

There were mixed feelings about this. At the one extreme there was the committed and uncritical fan; at the other was the refusenik epitomized by the character Tom in Tom Murphy's play, *Conversations on a Homecoming*: 'The real enemy – the big one! – that we shall overcome, is the country-and-western system itself. Unyielding, uncompromising in its drive for total sentimentality. A sentimentality I say that would have us all an unholy herd of Sierra Sues, sad-eyed inquisitors, sentimental Nazis, fascists, sectarianists, black- and blue-shirted nationalists with spurs a janglin', all ridin' down the trail to Oranmore.'

Like it or not, Big Tom was a central element in the cultural formation of a majority of Irish people born between the Emergency and the Mary Robinson presidency. Some of those affected or afflicted were volunteers, but most were conscripts. Some people went to his gigs to 'square' a member of the opposite sex. Some, although claiming to hate the music, went because they liked to jive. Many truly loathed the music, while others regarded it with an arched eyebrow. But, no matter how you heard it, the music seeped into your soul.

It was difficult to tell if Big Tom was for real or not. He was a strange phenomenon to look at – a mountain of a man with blond hair, dressed in incongruously colourful clothes, who sang a succession of odd songs without saying much besides, rarely communicating at all other than by means of the occasional theatrical wink. Apart from the clothes and the guitar, he looked as if he would have much happier behind the wheel of a Massey Ferguson.

But there was, too, a sense of mystery about it all, a suggestion of a ritualistic celebration of something felt at a very slightly deeper level. The mood was always carefree, even raucous, but the songs were all about pain and loss – so much so that it became funny. He called himself once 'a singer of sad songs'. He said: 'We're a sentimental race of people . . . We've had a lot of trouble down the years, so maybe we have reason for it.'

Big Tom had been born plain Tom McBride, in Castleblaney, County Monaghan, probably early in the 1930s. He left school at 14, got his first job working on a neighbouring farm for five shillings a week. He spent a decade or so going between Monaghan, Scotland and London, eventually settling down to a mix of farming, steel-erecting and music. In the early 1960s, Tom began playing with a local group called the Fincairn Ceili Band, performing mostly at dinner dances and weddings. He was the rhythm guitarist, singing the odd song, but eventually became the lead singer, singing a range of songs about love and exile that he'd picked up on his travels. His first hit was 'Gentle Mother', a country dirge about a dead mother. Tom had first heard it sung in London a decade before.

Country music Irish-style was to acquire a specific context as the folk music of a generation traumatized by involuntary emigration, and without any other means of expressing itself. Through the 1960s and 1970s, pop co-existed alongside this odd Irish hybrid, seeming to articulate the dichotomy of fear and hope that characterized the Lemass era and its messy aftermath. Pop became the voice of optimism and forgetting; 'Country 'n' Irish' that of apprehension and remembering.

The problem with Big Tom was not so much that he was shite, although he was in a way. The problem was that, underneath what he did there was the shadow of something else, something that might have been great if he had had the vision to excavate it and his audience had the intuition to demand it. The ironic response the music engendered was not without basis: there was the makings of something good rattling just below the surface. Had there been a Shane MacGowan happening along, capable of giving the music a root in the arse, who knows what might have come of it.

It would be a mistake to overlook the fact that it was in the 1980s, when emigration started up once again, that Daniel O'Donnell emerged to become an international star. His oeuvre owed something to 'Country 'n' Irish', but it lacked roughage and Daniel thought irony was a pill you took with your breakfast.

A few years after the ballroom boom died down, an American country singer called Garth Brooks started coming to Ireland for occasional performances. Brooks sang of a pain that was manageable and shallow. His voice did not penetrate like Bono's or Sinéad's. He allowed a little of the pain to show itself, but also enabled it to be covered over in a coat of sugary syrup. Within no time at all he had sold 500,000 albums in Ireland alone, a level of sales unequalled in any other market.

The truth of this phenomenon, which has never been named, is that Brooks appealed to the pop kids of the 1960s, for whom 'Country 'n' Irish' had had an attraction that they were loath to own up to. Now they were finding themselves experiencing a new appetite for sentimentality as they accompanied their own children to the airport. Brooks told a tale that few were willing to admit to: that just under the surface of the Irish psyche lay a melancholia that sought a particular form of expression. But, because of the 1970s backlash against country music, no Irish artist was at that time capable of meeting the needs of a generation caught between a fragile optimism and the renewed plausibility of despair.

People thought Big Tom was thick, perhaps because he looked thick. But he was a lot smarter than most of those who thought him unintentionally funny. There's a story about Mick Jagger, who used to visit Castleblaney in the 1970s, asking Tom for his autograph after seeing him signing for a gaggle of young women whom Jagger had first supposed would be more interested in himself. Jagger proffered a beermat and Big Tom, studying him carefully, enquired, 'Who'll I make it out to?'

'Mick Jagger, man!'

Tom regarded him carefully. 'Aye,' said he, 'an' you look like him too.'

23 Ray MacSharry

Perhaps the most tragic circumstance of the modern era for Irish society was that Ray MacSharry declined to make himself available to become Taoiseach. Having, by general agreement, almost single-handedly rescued the Irish economy from perdition in the late 1980s, he disappeared off to Brussels, where he spent a term as Ireland's EU Commissioner. Whenever speculation started up about the possibility of him returning to lead his party and his country, Ray slapped it down.

Back in 1987, following an election in which Fianna Fáil had issued mixed messages about its intentions, MacSharry became Minister for Finance in Charles Haughey's minority government. Haughey himself clearly didn't really know what to do about an economy with which several recent administrations, including two of his own, had achieved nothing but to make things worse. Haughey, in an attempt to differentiate Fianna Fáil from the outgoing lot with their talk of 'fiscal rectitude', had spoken vaguely during the campaign about 'developmental policies', giving the impression that there was a kinder, gentler way of snatching the country from the icy grip of death. But MacSharry was having none of it.

With his slightly stern air and what Olivia O'Leary called his 'Transylvanian good looks', MacSharry conveyed the right blend of reassurance and reserve. He didn't mince his words and, though we whimpered a little in our hair shirts, Mac made us feel safe. Rolling up his sleeves as we looked on in apprehension, he gripped the economy by the scruff of the neck and, in a few short if painful years, shook it into a better shape than it had even been in before.

MacSharry came from a working stock family in Sligo town. In 1988, a year into the term as Minister for Finance in which his zero-tolerance of budgetary excess would pave the way for the Celtic Tiger, he gave an interview to *Magill* magazine in which he spoke eloquently of the values he'd grown up with. In one quote that reads like a Bruce Springsteen song, he recalled the MacSharry family's first new car: 'One of the most distinctive memories I have is the first new car bought by my father. I was ten or eleven at the time. It was a Ford Prefect, EI 5043, and we were trading in a Baby Ford, IZ 3534, at Gilbride's Garage. The night before, I was with my father and my brother Louis when we counted out the money – three times – before going to bed. £230. And it was billions as far as we were concerned.'

When he took on the stewardship of the national finances in 1987, qualities of thrift, frugality and familiarity with life's harsh realities, which had attached themselves to him in the tough years of his childhood in 1940s' Sligo, stood also to the country. It was not easy, back then, to implement cuts in health, education and social welfare. But MacSharry pulled it off because he possessed a moral authority that exuded from personal connectedness to the reality of Irish life. He was not an ideologue seeking to impose an agenda. Nor, despite his ominous nickname – Mac the Knife – did he seek out easy targets. To the extent that human nature and reality will ever allow, the pain was evenly and fairly spread.

Even if you take the view that there has been a degree of exaggeration of MacSharry's role in the rejuvenation of the Irish economy in the 1990s, it is inconceivable that the disaster that befell us in the Noughties could have happened had he been anywhere in the building.

MacSharry is still hale and hearty, a strong, handsome man, only twenty years or so older than the present generation of Irish leaders. In cultural and ideological terms, however, a millennium separates him from the pampered generation that inherited his efforts in the 1990s.

Back in '88, the voiceless were the outrightly poor. But, although they suffered along with everyone else, they did not do so disproportionately – perhaps the greatest tribute that can be made to Ray MacSharry's integrity as a leader and as a man. Today the truly poor have battalions of spokespersons, and the voiceless are those who have just a little to lose: those who own their own houses and perhaps an apartment in the centre of town in anticipation of their children going to college later on, the people who maybe bought their first brand-new car in the past decade. A generation ago, such people did not need spokespersons because the political leadership came from their ranks and therefore saw the world as they did. But now they are the truly voiceless people in a society responding largely to cant and humbug, in which it is no longer possible to observe without controversy the obvious fact that wealth should be generated by effort and creativity, rather than by stock-jobbery and sleight-of-hand.

It is well we may rant and rave and gnash our teeth on account of losing the greatest Taoiseach we never had.

24 Jack Charlton

During those halcyon days of the Charlton Era, the Manager seemed constantly to be repeating the refrain: 'A nation of three-and-a-half million people cannot win the World Cup.' His intention, obviously, was to dampen down the growing public expectation that was to leave the widest street in Europe completely empty during more than one unforgettable encounter with one of the great sides of world football. Jack, of course, could not have been expected to know that Ireland is not a nation of three-and-a-half million people, but a nation of 75 million people dispersed throughout the world. And because Jack was a Brit, we were much too polite, what with all the baggage attaching to this insight, to bring up the matter.

Charlton brought possibly unprecedented joy into the lives of Irish citizens, at home and abroad. Often it seemed as if he had been sent from on high to cancel out every evil deed his countrymen had perpetrated in Ireland, and he certainly left the balance sheet a lot healthier when he eventually departed.

But therein also lay the problem with Jack: his Englishness was both the greatest asset he offered Ireland and also his fatal limitation. He was accomplished in an art form that was not indigenous to Ireland, but which had come to be a key medium in which we sought to express our sense of having arrived in the world. He came to Ireland with modest expectations, and in the end seemed astonished by what he had managed to stir up. Far more effectively than any native son, he had awoken the Irish to the possibility of success. And yet, neither he nor almost anyone else seemed to look beyond the prospect of a modest achievement.

One man who seemed to sense that much more was possible was Roy Keane, who would end his international career in a distressing little drama at the 2002 World Cup in Japan. Perhaps there are those who remain convinced that what concerned Roy Keane in Saipan was the quality of the facilities. But, as he was to make clear as the years passed, what he was really seeking to express was the frustration of someone who had grown to see his own dream come true, wanted to make it available to the country he loved, and, though convinced that more was possible, found himself confronted and confounded at every turn by the ineluctable pathology of losing. 'Win or lose,' he would derisively remark on a radio programme a few years later, 'hit the booze.'

Perhaps the Roy Keane saga carried also signifiers of a frustration that goes deep into the Irish psyche – a feeling buried under the weight of centuries of self-loathing that we might actually be as good as anyone else, and yet are expected, and therefore expect ourselves, to be delighted about getting knocked out in the quarter-finals. Perhaps Keane's response was some kind of existential roar of frustration at the idea that not only do our dreams always seem to get short-circuited, but the entire edifice we construct around our endeavours appears to make this inevitable.

The Irish attraction to soccer has long been more than an infatuation with the novelty of a global sport. Deep in the warped culture of late-twentieth-century Ireland, it was a form of subversion. There was a sense for us then that it provided a form of liberation from the weight of authority represented by GAA leaders, clergy, teachers and self-appointed cultural gurus who told us what being 'Irish' could mean and what it could not mean. It wasn't that we were actively rebelling against the re-Gaelicization of our cultural horizons, but rather that this process, for all that we may have supported or engaged with it, could not touch some other part of us that still needed to be nurtured: the colonized part, the part that remained incapable of expression in any identifiably indigenous code.

It was perhaps inevitable that soccer would become a vehicle for the unashamed expression of our post-colonial imagination, a sort of surrendering to that which, in other contexts, the national project of de-Anglicization sought to eliminate. Once you've been colonized, invaded, violated, you ever after need two distinct forms of self-expression. One is indigenous, a way of telling yourself who you still are. It needs to be of yourself, for yourself, by yourself, yourself alone. The other needs to be Other, of the outside, a means of saying to the rest of the world: I/we are still human, still living, still here; I/we can do what you can do (almost just as well, at least not as badly as you would expect). We are not as shite as we have been led to believe! Usually this means of expressing ourselves to the external will have been received from the violator, and will provide a way for the violated to seek the approval of he who has tried to persuade him that he is nothing. The two forms, obviously, operate at cross purposes. The very act of participating in something indigenous, however necessary this may be in one sense, validates the violator's poor opinion in another. And by succeeding at the other, I/we affirm a part of our own dread that we may no longer be fully ourselves. We cannot win, but please don't say it aloud.

This paradox defines the relationship between Gaelic games and soccer in Irish life and society. Gaelic games are the means of affirming ourselves to ourselves, a way of expressing our relief at the departure of the invader and celebrating his banishment. Soccer is the expression of that part of us that remains colonized, however long the visitors have departed. Soccer is the means we have unconsciously chosen to say, 'Look, there is no need to be disappointed in our progress! Look, we can be like you after all! Look, we have not fallen back into barbarism! We are something, in spite of ourselves!'

The difficulty is that the very urge to demonstrate our capability is matched by a defeatism implanted also by the invader, which tells us that, no, we cannot ever win. What we crave more than anything is possible through soccer, but *that*, because it belongs to our former abuser, is infected for us with a pathology of losing. The very means we had found to express our desire to be as good as anyone has an in-built mechanism preventing us from becoming that which we crave to be.

Before Charlton, whenever the Irish national team took the field, the best expectations of the nation resided with the prospect of another 'moral victory'. This was when you got sixty-four kinds of DNA kicked out of you but you still did not lie down. You might be beaten 15-nil, but if you hit the side-netting in the closing minutes, that was 'a moral victory', a sign that there remained a glimmering spark at the core of the unbending spirit of the Irish, and a portent of greatness still to come.

The incredible success of the national football team under Jack Charlton in the late 1980s and early '90s, revealed itself in retrospect as a rehearsal of the Celtic Tiger economic miracle of the decade that followed – a glittering success that for a cosmic moment promised to wipe out nearly a century of failure. Both phenomena were managed, supervised and controlled by foreigners; and, more pertinently, both were based on a product that might be termed non-indigenous.

There is, then, a remarkable similarity between our responses in the respective arenas of industry and sport, and soccer tells the story more clearly than other sports. In both soccer and industrial policy, we like to leave it to outsiders. It is not that we lack self-belief – indeed, when someone comes in and takes charge, we find self-belief in open-top busloads. But we are poor self-starters, and especially poor at seeing ourselves in an area of expression or activity we perceive as belonging to peoples who can exude self-confidence without a barrelful of ale.

These are the facts of what Jack Charlton stirred up in us. The tragedy was not that he failed, but that he succeeded beyond his own wildest dreams, and thereby made visible what was possible but at the same time unrealizable.

Not once during his years as manager of the Irish football team was Jack Charlton asked: 'Could a nation of 75 million people win the World Cup?' If we had only had the belief to put it like that, he might have said 'yes', and who knows what might have happened?

25 Gerry Adams

Everyone knows Gerry Adams was not just 'in' the IRA but in it at a pretty senior level. Innumerable times it has been written that for many years he was Commander of the Belfast Brigade of the Provisional IRA. He denies it, but has not sued anyone for what, if it is untrue, must surely strike him as a grave slur on his character. Books have been written linking him to some of the ugliest operations of the IRA – for example, the 'disappearance' of Jean McConville in 1972. Jean McConville was a young widow who came to the aid of a young British soldier dying in the street. For this she was abducted by the IRA, taken to a secluded place, shot once in the head and buried on the spot. It would be many years before her body was found, accidentally, by a man who came across a scrap of clothing while out playing with his child.

Gerry Adams told Jean McConville's family that he had nothing to do with these events, that he was in prison at the time. This was untrue. Everyone knew that he was the senior commander in Belfast when this murder was carried out.

The great fiction of the 'republican movement' has been the idea of a separation between its political wing, Sinn Féin, and the 'freedom fighters' in the IRA. Everyone knows this was a necessary fiction to avoid imprisonment. When the conflict was brought to an end by the Good Friday Agreement of 1998, many republicans

came forward to admit to their former freedom-fighting activities. Martin McGuinness, for example, admitted that he had been a senior figure in the IRA and took responsibility for the pain and grief he had inflicted on so many. He refused to go into details but still it was felt that he had gone some way towards atoning for any wrongs he had committed.

But not Gerry. Clinging to the fiction, Adams insisted that he had never been in the IRA. In fact, he told Gay Byrne on *The Late Late Show* that he had never so much as thrown a stone during a riot. He was a politician, not a freedom fighter. Mind you, he did not condemn freedom fighting – there had, after all, been a war on. It's just that he hadn't been a fighter himself.

In the immediate wake of the Good Friday settlement, this didn't seem to matter. Adams had been a key figure in the delicate process by which peace was achieved. Indeed, as a senior republican who was prepared to risk his own safety by talking the republican movement around, he might well be deemed the most critical figure in that process. For a short time he was something of a hero. Commentators who had previously attacked Gerry Adams and all his works and pomp now acknowledged his statesmanlike qualities. Very few people in the Republic any longer believed that there had been any 'war', but were glad that, however it was to be described, it was now over. The voters of the Republic had even agreed to dismantle their own constitutional aspiration to the eventual unity of their country by agreeing to amend Articles 2 and 3 of the Irish Constitution, Bunreacht na hÉireann, just to stop the Provos slaughtering people. More and more nationalists in the Republic were coming around to the view that the whole thing had been an unnecessary exercise in egotism and viciousness by a generation of Northern thugs who sought to appropriate the national flag and the history it signified so as to legitimize what was really no more than a squalid turf war pursued by ruthless criminals. After years of extending tacit support to the 'armed struggle', many people had become persuaded that, although the Brits and the unionists had much to answer for, the IRA's response had been utterly dispro-portionate and deeply immoral. After thirty years of conflict and more than 3,000 deaths, the Provos had achieved nothing more than had been on the table at the beginning. Now they were prepared to exchange all the alleged principles on which they had fought their 'war' for a few seats in an assembly that could have been agreed nearly three decades previously if they had been prepared to be reasonable. They had fought for 'freedom' and settled for power.

Nevertheless, in the early days of the new-found peace, people were prepared to indulge Gerry Adams in his fictive endeavours. People understood that it was sometimes necessary to be less than totally truthful in the interests of peace and harmony. Because everyone had been so anxious to ensure that the peace was main-tained, it was considered that a certain latitude should be accorded to Gerry's pretences. If he had just kept his mouth shut, people might have been able to live with it.

But in his every public utterance as a politician, Gerry adopted a high moral tone about corruption, criminality and wrongdoing. He seemed not to understand the contradictions of his banging on about the alleged criminality of others when he refused to admit to his own past. He berated bankers, freeloading politicians and paedophile priests, demanding that heads be delivered on plates and keys be cast off the edges of cliffs. He did not blink once at the irony of it all. Adopting the ideological palette of a left-liberal politician, he pontificated about equality and women's rights. He seemed to have forgotten all about Jean McConville and her truncated life as a woman and mother. He attacked the continuing campaigns of irredentist republicans as though he had never fired a shot in anger in his life. Even when he was implicated in a controversy in which his own brother was accused of abusing his daughter, who came out to say that she had told Gerry all about it many years before, Gerry did not break his stride in demanding the resignations of bishops who had failed to blow the whistle on pervert priests.

All this has had a gruesome effect on the stomach of modern Ireland. People could not help finding it strange that a man who had, to their certain knowledge, been up to his oxters in the blood of innocents, should now presume to be regarded as the conscience of the Irish nation. It made people want to throw up. It sent their moral compasses crazy. But still they had to listen to it, because Gerry was now a fully constitutional politician whose past was nobody's business but his own.

26 Bono

U2 are more important to the story of contemporary Ireland than most commentaries seek to suggest. The standard analysis remains doggedly on the surface, celebrating the wondrousness of the idea that a rock'n'roll band originating in Ireland could possibly be regarded as the best in the world.

Little credence is given to the idea that U2, in their progress through the world, have unveiled a kind of secret history of Ireland. A deeper examination of their own history reveals a community of individuals who were somehow able to transcend the exterior climate of negativity and reaction, and to drive their receptors deep into the culture whence they emerged, acquiring a shamanic capacity to plumb the interior reservoirs of Irish creativity and genius, creating in the process a parallel dramatization of Ireland on the world stage.

In the 1990s, this became deeply infectious for their own people. Even that prevailing superficial idea of their world-conquering adventuring seemed to creep into the soul of their native land, provoking in their fellow countrymen a counter-intuitive 'Me too?' followed by a defiant 'Why not?'

But if we are to give them credit for in part inspiring the national reinvigoration that became world-famous as the Celtic Tiger, then we must also consider the possibility that, somewhere in the U2

story there was also a portent of the unwinding of that miracle in the late Noughties.

When people find fault with U2, it usually tends to be about the extra-curricular stuff: Bono's charity campaigning or the cartoon persona he's fashioned for the stadium that is the modern mass media world. The first time U2 got on the cover of *Time*, over two decades ago, the 'Rock's Hottest Ticket' headline provided their fellow citizens with an opportunity for an orgy of reflected glory-ing. Nowadays this kind of thing happens so often, we realize that Bono has not just outstripped the rest of the rock'n'roll pack and become far bigger than his own band, but has left his native country behind as well. This provokes a complex reaction in his fellow countrymen, which often comes out as resentment. And this, again, causes us to miss the main plot.

Much as it irritates so many people who insist that 'it's only rock'n'roll', Bono has for some time been going bravely where no celebrity spokesman for his generation had gone before, earning considerable international respect for himself and his motivations, and offering an answer to the niggling question about whether rock'n'roll can move beyond its Dionysian obsession with sex, drugs and other false forms of freedom. These ambitions derive, whether we like it or not, from the Irish historical experience of wretchedness and want. Part of the reason Bono's evangelicalism provokes such antagonism in Anglo-Saxon culture is that the experience he calls on has far more in common with the black societies in which rock'n'roll emerged than it has with the 'white' world to which Ireland ostensibly belongs.

The real problem, strangely, is with the music. In the beginning, U2 created a soundtrack that, in its innocence and innovation, retrospectively revealed itself as containing a prophecy of the shifts in Irish culture and fortunes. But then, deep in the 1990s, as soon as the prophecy began to take hold, something happened. It is as if U2, having discovered their essence, were struck down by the same condition that had affected their native country in their childhoods: a kind of retreating into a settled view of themselves, a solidifying around their own essence with a view to maintaining their brand and position.

The band's two early-2000s albums, *All That You Can't Leave Behind* and *How to Dismantle an Atomic Bomb*, were disappointing for anyone who had truly tuned into U2's mission. Confusingly, they sounded like great rock'n'roll albums should sound, even a bit like great U2 albums. But they didn't sound like the albums U2 should have been making at the age they were, in a sequence defined from *Boy* to *Achtung Baby*.

The 1990s' in-between albums, *Zooropa* and *Pop*, were essentially scrapbook albums of various experimental elements traceable to the revolution that had occurred in the band's imagination at the time of the extraordinary 1991 opus *Achtung Baby*. But the subsequent albums cannot be excused on this basis, since they were produced at leisure and after considerable contemplation. In an odd way, they reflected the complacency and self-congratulation that crept into Irish life in the early years of the new millennium, when everyone became so pleased with themselves as to forget about the necessity for constant regeneration.

Of course, the idea that there was anything wrong with these albums may seem mystifying to many people. They were massively successful, and this is difficult to argue with. The trouble is that the ethic governing both these albums seemed to be more about affirming U2's role as the world's foremost rock'n'roll band than about the U2 mission as understood from the beginning.

U2 always promised more. They promised meaning and mission and undertook to liberate rock'n'roll from its modern obsession with the material. They said the world could go far if it listened to what they said. They gathered up a ragged medium and sought to reintroduce it to its own roots. They demanded of pop no less than that it grow up. Having started as pop-illiterates, they acquired an awesome competence which they emphasized was for an exalted purpose. They seemed to represent a defiance of imposed cultural notions and yet utilized these notions as the very fabric of their creativity. There was something here about redemption, about taking back the devil's music, about wrestling the guitar from the grasp of the dark angel, about demonstrating some connection between inspiration and faith, reason and humility, love and rigour, hope and desire. It wasn't just about giving God a good guitar sound, but about showing how some hitherto implausible connections could be extended into the stratosphere of the pop imagination, infiltrating the secular consciousness with something beyond the hip and the harmless. It was about giving a voice to things we all felt, underneath, but lacked permission to speak.

Those ambitions, though constantly implicit, tended to move ahead of the band, a vaguely defined but nevertheless deeply-held set of aspirations that promised something extraordinary for those who stuck around. With *The Joshua Tree* and *Achtung Baby*, there was a sense that U2 were about to reach out and touch their very reason for being, and perhaps in doing so define anew the uncreated conscience of their own race. But the target kept moving and, more worryingly, U2 appeared not to notice. They kept talking about how music is more than diversion and about the possibilities of the medium to make a difference beyond the dance floor. And they kept on making music that seemed to miss the point of their own existence. That music was unquestionably U2, but when you took off the wrapping there was nothing there but the sentimental repetition of the unanswered question.

This crisis went largely unnoticed. Perhaps, though it seems unlikely, it went unnoticed even by the band-members themselves. Indeed, because the problem sounded as if it had arisen from an increasing atomization of the band, perhaps the very process of undoing conspired also to conceal the difficulty. The thing about U2 had always been that the whole was much greater than the parts. But the music they produced as they hit middle age conveyed a sense that what they embodied was no longer a passion born of friendship and ambition, but four individual forms of craftsmanship acquired in togetherness and now rapidly diverging. There was, in the predictable grammar of their newer songs, in the adherence to fashion and formula rather than the forbidden, a vaguely detectable hint that what each of the four was now contributing was less defined by the internal dynamic that had made the band great. U2 had become, to an extent, trapped in the codes they had started out trying to subvert. They no longer appeared able to access the collective recklessness of the early days.

This is what made *No Line on the Horizon* such a welcome arrival in 2009, a recording that at once consolidated U2's position as the world's great rock'n'roll band and reasserted their core mission to remind us that everything we 'know' is wrong. In a subtle way, without disturbing the core U2 sound or sensibility, it took us somewhere new. Bono was singing better on this album than he had for a long time, and seemed again to be at home in the sound the rest of the band were creating around him.

Perhaps, again, it is prophetic. Perhaps, for those who seek to look deeper, it is the continuation of that secret history of Irish culture. Perhaps. We can only hope that history is capable of holding the tune.

27 Gerry McGuinness

Two major events more or less coincided with the launch of the *Sunday World* in 1973. For one thing, that was the year that Fine Gael returned to power after a hiatus of seventeen years. The Liam Cosgrave-led coalition would become notorious as a reactionary and miserly administration, accelerating Ireland's slide from the optimism of the Lemass years into the heart of a decade dominated by oil crises and the spreading radiation from the violence across the border. The other event was the retirement of Eamon de Valera, at the end of his second seven-year term as President of the Republic. But by 1973, instead of a nation defined by happy maidens and athletic youths, it was coming to be defined by comely boys like Marc Bolan and David Bowie pouting out from *Top of the Pops*. The firesides of the nation were alive not with the serene wisdom of old age, but the weekly theatrical deconstructions of existing values on *The Late Late Show*.   *See Gay Byrne!*

For decades, the Irish Sunday newspaper market had been dominated by two broadsheet titles, the *Sunday Independent*, and Dev's own paper, the *Sunday Press*, which had gained circulation through being sold at church gates. Now there was a new kid on the block.

The very first issue of the *Sunday World* hit the streets on 25 March 1973. It was planned as a dummy run, and was being launched on a shoestring, but publishers Gerry McGuinness and Hugh McLaughlin were so pleased with the results that they had 200,000 copies printed and circulated. The first *Sunday World* sold out.

The main story that day was about the hunt for two Belfast girls who had lured a couple of British soldiers to their deaths in a flat on the Antrim Road. There was also a front-page piece speculating about reports that Patrick Hillery might return from his job as European Commissioner to succeed de Valera as president. The front-page pin-up girl, dressed in a striped, woollen mini-skirt, was a young actress called Jeananne Crowley. Inside were more pin-ups and full-page colour photos of, incongruously, pop heart-throb Donny Osmond and the new Cosgrave coalition cabinet. Although calling itself a newspaper, the *Sunday World* was really a magazine. It carried snippets about music, TV, films, gossip and fashion. There was a sports section and a few lightweight opinion columns. Politics was not a priority. In an early edition of the newspaper, in a piece about 'the sexiest men in Irish politics', the leading feminist Nuala Fennell nominated the new Minister for Foreign Affairs, Garret FitzGerald, despite the fact 'his appearance at times reminds me of Noddy'. PR guru Terry Prone owned up to 'a passion for Justin Keating'.

The editor of the paper was Joe Kennedy, an ex-folkie poached from Independent newspapers, he was a thoughtful and experienced journalist, once in the running for the editorship of the *Sunday Independent*. His favourite journalists were left-wing radicals like James Cameron and Claud Cockburn. The assistant editor was Kevin Marron, who had come from the *Sunday Press*. The paper also boasted one of Ireland's most experienced and respected journalists, Liam MacGabhann, and a handful of interesting newcomers, including a young Derryman called

Eamonn McCann. McCann was a socialist and political firebrand. But he wrote beautifully and passionately about politics, pop culture and the odd relationship between the two Irelands separated by the border.

To begin with, the *Sunday World* was actually a good newspaper, and then it got even better. It was at once radical and lively, containing campaigning journalism alongside harmless but entertaining commentary by people like Gay Byrne and Father Brian D'Arcy.

Under Kennedy, and later under his successor, Kevin Marron, the paper continued to publish intelligent and important journalism about prison conditions, discrimination, homeless children and so forth. It also led the way in opening up discussions about taboo subjects like homosexuality, incest and drugs. Sales were going through the roof. By 1981, the paper was selling 350,000 copies, way ahead of its nearest competitor, the *Sunday Press*.

Meanwhile, Hughie McLaughlin had been bought out by Tony O'Reilly, which meant that the *Sunday World* had become part of the Independent Group, owned by Tony O'Reilly. Gerry McGuinness, too, came to an arrangement whereby both his newspaper and himself were absorbed into the Independent Group.

Although O'Reilly was clearly delighted with the continuing success of his new acquisition, he never sought an input into the editorial direction of the paper, and according to one senior journalist, never as much as set foot in the office of the paper back then.

When Kevin Marron suffered a brain haemorrhage in 1981 (he would later die in a plane crash), he was replaced by Colin McClelland, who was preoccupied by populist ideas about crime and vandalism, which he described as 'the evil and obscene cancer gnawing away at the roots of our society'. Before long, the *Sunday*

World had come to be better known for its fearless exposés on 'massage parlours' than for possibly anything else.

There was a time when the *Sunday World* defined not just popular journalism Irish-style but may actually have been creating an idiosyncratically Irish tabloid sensibility by which Irish life and Irish ways might have been treated in a manner reflecting the country's development as an independent but connected culture on the edge of Western civilization. This didn't happen. The primary blame for this must be laid at the door of Gerry McGuinness. It was he who resisted the model of journalism pursued from the beginning by Joe Kennedy, which had arguably laid the groundwork for the early phenomenal success of the *Sunday World*. It took a number of years for the *Sunday World* to begin showing the signs of becoming the reactionary newspaper it is today, and in this drift it lit the way for other Irish tabloids to follow. In the end, the Irish 'redtops' became carbon copies of English ones. The model established in the early days by Kennedy, Marron and others was supplanted by the generic Fleet Street model, albeit without the irony and the wit.

As the paper softened, sales dipped, but not sufficiently to change anything. It continued to sell in truckloads. Having hooked readers with good journalism, the *Sunday World* moderated their tastes and expectations and supplied them with a diet that was cheaper to produce and less taxing on their brains.

The *Sunday World* set the tone and template for future Irish tabloids, like the *Star*, and for British redtops devising their Oirish editions. Consequently, and harsh as it may seem, Gerry McGuinness must therefore answer on Judgement Day for the present-day *Evening Herald*.

28 Mary Robinson

When Mary Robinson ran for the presidency of Ireland in 1990, she sold herself as someone who wanted to restore national self-confidence and create healing between various entities on the island: Protestants and Catholics, of course; men and women; country and city.

As an arch-feminist, born the daughter of two Mayo doctors, she was somewhat behind the eight ball to begin. She had endeared herself to unionist opinion by taking a stance on the Anglo-Irish Agreement, resigning from the Labour Party in protest. Other than making southern Catholics more suspicious of her, this had no effect on anything. And now she hoped to persuade an electorate comprising 95 per cent Catholics to make her President of the Republic.

Robinson was respected but not particularly likable. She had been a prominent lawyer, involved in numerous high-profile cases involving 'women's issues'. People thought her somewhat strident in a posh sort of way. She came across as a member of the Anglo-Irish aristocracy rather than as a daughter of Mayo. She spoke in a slightly fruity accent, and dressed like a nun in mufti, nodding all the time as she spoke. She had a stern outward appearance. There wasn't much crack to her. The fact that she looked and sounded like pure-bred Dublin 4 pretty much ruled out her chances of garnering votes anywhere else.

Robinson said that she wanted to 'change' Ireland, but change it into something that, she implied, it wished to become. She sought to reassure people that she was not some left-wing Trojan horse, some fire-eating feminist dragon who, if she won, would seek to claim a famous victory over 'the forces of conservatism'. One of the senior Labour Party people involved in her campaign afterwards described it as being like a train with lots of different carriages filled with different kinds of people. The trick was not to let people in any one carriage know who was in the others. To have any hope of being elected, she would have to gain votes not just from the left-liberal constituency, but from across the spectrum, all over the country.

More than six months before the campaign would rightly begin, Robinson began her work in Allihies in west Cork, and afterwards travelled the length and breadth of Ireland trying to overcome her disadvantages and persuade 'ordinary' Irish people to vote for her. She did not slap any backs, but she clasped the sweaty hand of middle Ireland. She forced a smile and kissed babies. Her rhetoric was inclusive and almost warm. She said that there did not have to be winners or losers, there did not have to be sides. By fighting against the perceived conservative forces in Irish society, she had come to appreciate the nature of those forces: that they were not merely the preserve of a diehard minority, but an essential part of the equilibrium of the society. Conservatism and liberalism, she explained, were not for her exterior forces, but intrinsic parts of herself, of her own experience and outlook, just as they were parts of all Irish people. 'I'm a Catholic from Mayo,' she said. 'So there's nothing about *that* Ireland that I don't know. So it's me. I understand it from within and I want to develop it on, but in a way that one would want to develop oneself, almost. I don't repudiate as much as want to coax along into a different mould.'

Afterwards, there were assiduous efforts to reinterpret her victory as emblematic of a narrow range of orthodoxies. When the writers came over from *Time* and *Vanity Fair*, they were facilitated by Robinson proponents in writing simplistic analyses of what was going on. The country, which just four years earlier had rejected divorce, the world was told, had had a sudden and dramatic change of heart. The 'old' Ireland was in retreat. The Irish were now ready to join the modern world.

What this ignored was that most of the people on the Robinson train espoused a multiplicity of complex and often contradictory views about everything. Some of them, for example, had no problem with divorce but abhorred abortion. Some of them were simply sick of the old tribal politics. Some of them were female chauvinists. Some of them were men who thought that electing a woman President would be a nice exercise in window-dressing. And so on.

The rinsed-down reason we elected Robinson was that we suddenly became drunk on the possibility that we could. In truth, her election was more of a gesture than a symbol. She won at a time when people were beginning to think it might be fun to overturn the party political bandwagons. Robinson succeeded in presenting herself as unthreatening to a sufficiency of people to enable her to sneak past the post on the second count. We had no idea what it might mean, or how on earth it could be deemed to mean anything, but somehow we decided that it was better to do it than not do it. In this sense, her election was emblematic of the modernizing-cum-liberalizing ethic with which she had come to be identified, representing a form of change which was purely reactive, which has no real announcement to make but simply wanted to denounce what already existed.

Having promised to reinvent the presidency, Robinson appeared to use it as a platform for her own advancement and greater glory.

The very fact that she had been elected was enough, it seemed. Nearing the end of her term of office, she pulled plant to take up a big job in the UN. So much for her desire to reinvigorate the self-confidence of the Irish people.

In the end, the Irish people were left wondering what, other than the career of Mary Robinson, it had all been about. What had changed other than that the person going around opening gymkhanas was a woman rather than a man. It wasn't just that the whole thing had been an elaborate con-trick to get Robinson elected, but that it had been an elaborate con-trick that created an impression of 'change' and 'progress', when really nothing much was changing or progressing at all.

If this was not sufficient to display Mrs Robinson in her true colours, an episode that occurred some three years later would put an end to any remaining doubts. Robinson, now United Nations High Commissioner for Human Rights, was speaking on International Women's Day. By now she had been replaced as President by another woman, Mary McAleese, an entirely different class of individual by any standard.

'Apparently,' Robinson told her receptive audience of like-minded sisters, 'there are small boys in Ireland who are complaining to their mothers, "Why can't I grow up to be President?" That seems to me to be an excellent experience for small boys in Ireland.'

Finally, it was all laid bare. The grandiose rhetoric of inclusiveness had fallen away and we were left with the spectacle of one of the pettiest chauvinists the nation had ever nurtured gloating because, as a result of her glorious endeavours, little boys could no longer hope to become the first citizen of the Republic. Sisters, what a triumph!

In Robinson's defence, it might be said that the remark was an attempt at a joke by someone with no sense of humour. But no –

underlying her words was a deeply disquieting hostility – even managing to exceed the standard everyday feminist rancour towards males. By virtue of being specifically directed at young boys, her words attained a new level of unwomanly malevolence.

Of course, deep down, very few of those who voted for her expected Robinson to be otherwise. None of it really meant anything. She had become the incarnation of values that we were instructed we had to adopt but in which most sensible people saw very little value. We liked the idea of having a President who represented 'liberal' ideas without having the right to express, still less implement, them. As President, we welcomed her necessary fudges and enforced silences, because they allowed us to have the name of modernity without having to work out what it might actually mean – in concrete Irish terms. She represented our unspoken desire to be perceived as liberal without surrendering the fabric of our existing society to a process of unravelling for which there seemed to be few rules or principles. In short, Mary Robinson did not turn the first sod on a new highway to the future; she cut the tape on a cul-de-sac into which we pulled to have a look at the map. And we're still there.

29 Louis Walsh

As the 1980s progressed and the emerging Irish rock'n'roll constituency began to come to terms with the fact that U2 were, really and truly, the biggest rock'n'roll band in the world, the disbelief and wonder provoked by this began to give way to a sense of national entitlement. Very quickly the conversation shifted to oscillating between backbiting about the fact that U2 were regarded as perhaps the least worthy of their generation of post-punk contenders and desultory debates about who would become 'the next U2'.

A couple of top-flight acts did manifest themselves, notably Sinéad O'Connor. But, generally speaking, the growing conventional wisdom that Dublin could come to be to the 1990s rock'n'roll imagination what Merseyside had been in the 1960s was a little thin on content. Various contenders came and went, but only U2 and O'Connor seemed to have staying power.

But then the future of Irish music declared itself. One night on *The Late Late Show*, following a discussion about the future of rural Ireland between a journalist, a priest and, for some reason, a female disc jockey, a bunch of daft-looking young fellas shambled on to the set. Rumour had it that it was some new wheeze of Louis Walsh, a showbiz impresario who had become prominent in the showband era. The word was that the new act would be a kind of Irish Take That. The obvious question was: why?

The bunch of young fellas called themselves Boyzone. They didn't sing that night, but instead mimed to a dance track. Everyone laughed uproariously at this evidence of Louis Walsh's hard neck. Nobody thought it remotely serious. But within months, Boyzone were one of the most successful music acts in the UK. In no time at all, the success of Boyzone was dwarfed by another Walsh-inspired sensation, Westlife, who seemed to turn everything they touched into gold.

Where once we were known as the Island of Saints and Scholars, Ireland is nowadays famous as the Nation of Boybands. Never was this truth so visible as during the celebrations to mark the onset of the third millennium, when it seemed that boybands had supplanted the entirety of Irish culture in the previous 1,000 years. The nation of Carolan and Ó Riada, the nation whose bardic culture had once been called 'the earliest voice from the dawn of West European civilization', the nation that had once given the world missionaries dedicated to painstaking calligraphy and Christian gratuitousness was now known globally as the producer of ambiguous-looking young men who could cavort to a beat created by a machine operated by a man from Mayo who had spent a lifetime studying the odds and watching for the main chance.

If ever there was a necessity for evidence of how the Irish nation had lost touch with itself, a video of the proceedings on the premier national television channel in the last hours of the second millennium would be enough to convey to an indefinitely extend-ing posterity our inability to explain anything about ourselves. Anyone who watched could hardly be surprised about anything that followed: the excess, the loss of the country's run of itself, the economic and psychic breakdown that followed hard on the indulgences of the Celtic Tiger.

Here we had a succinct proof of Jean Baudrillard's theory that time has started to go backwards, as the coverage cut from the boyband mediocrity on Merrion Square, where a New Year's concert was taking place, to the sad spectacle of the one-time king of the ballroom circuit, Joe Dolan, playing in Killarney, the whole thing suggesting not so much a celebration of the future as an attempt to drag posterity down to our level. Weirdly, the 'past' being focused upon was not the great sweep of time through the annals and battlefields and mass graves of Irish history, but Ireland's alleged strides in the world of popular entertainment in the previous forty years. More than that, what emerged from it was a strong sense of how post-Independence popular culture in Ireland had continued to slide backwards into its congenital rootlessness.

Even if he cannot be held completely responsible for this miasma of selective forgetfulness and remembered inferiority, Louis Walsh was so constantly at the scene of the crime(s) that he qualifies for special blame. Walsh had been one of the main players in the showband industry, which, for all its flaws, had at least the redeeming quality of innocence. The boyband craze of the Tiger years was indistinguishable from showband culture except that we at least had the decency to keep showbands to ourselves.

In their time and proper place, actually, showbands weren't anything like as bad as they're sometimes 'remembered'. Far more than Gay Byrne or Mary Robinson, people like Joe Dolan and the Drifters, Derek Dean and Billy Brown of The Freshmen, and Brendan Bowyer with the Royal Showband, revolutionized Irish attitudes to sexuality and freedom. It is, in a certain light, arguable that Big Tom was more central to the modernization of Irish society than the cumulative effects of the *Irish Times*, the Labour Party and the First Programme for Economic Expansion.

Louis Walsh was for a time manager of The Freshmen, one of the genuinely great bands of the showband era. He was therefore at the scene of the Big Bang of Irish popular culture, a spontaneous explosion of activity from a void of nothingness. When you factor in the deeply derivative nature of much of what passed for originality in early Irish rock'n'roll, it occurs that, in their own way, showbands were as creative as anyone. Certainly they were creative of excitement and abandon on a previously undreamt-of scale, and some show-band records, like The Royal's version of 'The Hucklebuck', and The Freshmen's version of 'Papa-Oom-Mow-Mow', can stand with anything in the past fifty years of Irish pop music.

But no argument of this kind can be mounted in defence of boybands, which came after a time when Ireland had shown itself capable of producing the finest and most creative musical artists in the world.

One of Westlife's hit singles, released at Christmas 1999, was a ditty called 'Seasons in the Sun', an English-language adaptation of the song 'Le Moribond' by the stunning Belgian singer-songwriter Jacques Brel. It had been a mega-hit back in the mid-1970s when recorded by one Terry Jacks, a truly awful recording, a mawkish, revolting excess of self-pity and frothy pathos, utterly devoid of Brelesque irony or self-parody. 'Goodbye Michelle', went the lyric, 'it's hard to die/When all the birds are singing in the sky.' To be fair, Terry Jacks knew that a capacity to tap into these darker feelings was the song's only 'redeeming' feature, and hammed it up for all it was worth. Westlife, on the other hand, didn't even appear to have noted this aspect of the song, which they sing as though it were 'Baa-baa Black Sheep'.

Louis Walsh had learned something dark and deadly in his showband days. He looked into the soul of his fellow man and figured out what it would be prepared to settle for. His refusal to carry this insight with him to the grave will not be easily forgiven.

30 Ian Paisley

Once, back in the 1970s, Paisley boasted of how John Hume had once turned to him in frustration and said, 'Paisley, you're just an Ulster Protestant.'

'I replied to Mr Hume: "I am glad that at last you have got the message. I am indeed an Ulster Protestant!"'

Although there has since been the bones of an accommodation between Southern nationalism and Paisley's tribe, the truth of the matter is that the condition of Ulster Protestantism is still as mystifying to most of those who live south of the border as it ever was. We just don't get it: their reciprocal ignorance of Southern nationalism, their rage against the Republic, their belligerence, their dogged insistence on being 'British' in defiance of geography and self-interest. Neither do we get the way they don't get us: their persistent prating about 'Rome rule', long after the fact. Their continuing condescension about the 'banana republic' and their ironic references to the 'Free State', even though their own little 'statelet' went to wrack and ruin while the Republic was going to Paradise and back. 'They try to explain Ian Paisley, but they don't understand,' the Big Fella elaborated to a meeting of his followers in Omagh in 1981. 'Ian Paisley is the incarnation of every Protestant Ulsterman here at this meeting tonight. I am only saying what you want me to say, what you want to hear.'

In a speech denouncing the latest joint initiative of the British and Irish governments, Big Ian criticized both Charles Haughey, Taoiseach of the Republic, and Humphrey Atkins, the Northern Ireland Secretary of State. The readings that night were from the Old Testament, the music was 'Rock of Ages'. A bystander's report described a scene of passionate intensity. When speaking, the Reverend Paisley delivered an improvised oration that transported his audience to new heights and new places in themselves. His arms flailed and the sweat poured off him. His voice rose in pitch and power, like a tenor coming to the climax of his final aria.

'We shall defend what is ours. We be determined men, come to do a task, and with God's almighty grace we will do it. I say to Charles Haughey, that son of an IRA gunman from Swatragh, that guardian of the IRA whose murderers have darkened sixty Fermanagh homes with death. Charlie Haughey, the Godfather of our intended destruction, the green aggressor, I say to you, Charlie Haughey, that you will never get your thieving, murderous hands on Ulster, because we are determined to fertilize the ground of Ulster with Protestant blood before we enter your priest-ridden banana republic.'

There have been many books, many articles and a multitude of broadcast documentaries produced about the 'troubles' on the island of Ireland over the past forty years. But not even the best among these efforts has come close to capturing the complex inter-flow of currents and forces, the undertows and whirlpools of this most incomprehensible of conflicts. This story is all but untellable, in part because the roots of the conflict extended to so many levels of Irish society, north and south. And yet, somehow, the mysterious nature of both the conflict and its eventual resolution are summarized in the personality of Ian Paisley, and the complex nature of his relationship with those inhabitants of the island who were not happy to call themselves British.

Not long ago, Ian Paisley was greatly feared by the people of the Republic – and not in an abstract sense. He was feared in the manner of a demonic force of nature whose tempers seemed to threaten on a scale that was godlike. He was the stuff of our nightmares, and not just the metaphorical, political kind. He was someone who had us crunching bolt upright in bed in the deadest hours, quaking under the thunderous bellow of his voice, recoiling from the fiery torches of his eyes and wiping his spittle from our fearful faces.

Fast forward to the Noughties, and Paisley had metamorphosed as though into our favourite uncle, a cheery broth of a boy who made us laugh inwardly at the ridiculousness of the idea that we had ever seen him differently. Even those of us who never met him in the flesh – who might even yet recoil from such a meeting for fear that he would revert to type in our presence – have come to, yes, love Paisley. The word is not too strong.

This change of heart did not occur for wholly political reasons, nor can its drifts and shifts be conveyed by psychological analysis. But if the story of recent Irish history can be comprehended at all, it is to be comprehended in the personality of Ian Paisley, and in his shifting relationships with the various political and human entities on the island.

Paisley belongs to a rare elite of political figures who have brought to politics the fullness of a strong personality and confronted history as though it were a little boy asking for more. The nearest equivalent produced in the Republic was Charles Haughey, but compared to Paisley, Haughey was, as Paisley always intuited, that little boy.

Only by understanding how we came to love Paisley can we begin to understand what has happened to ourselves. This is not comprehensible in terms of memoranda, discussion documents, declarations, still less of bombs, bullets and kneecappings. These were but the surface events of a drama that went to the core of the identities of the peoples on the island of Ireland in the second half of the 20th century.

The image of the 'Chuckle Brothers' conveys something of what has happened. We watched Ian Paisley and Martin McGuinness in the paroxysms of mirth brought on by their blossoming friendship, and something of the benign mystery of reconciliation came across. These men who used to hate and slander each other, now belly-laughed at each other's jokes. But this was more than an image of two men. It was an image from a culture that changed because of the complex interworkings of human personality as much as by the plodding and drudgery of politics. The Chuckle Brothers were the children of reinvented public desires, two men who stood for many more. The spectacle of their bodies trembling with laughter would not have been possible unless something enormous had shifted deep in the soul of Ireland. For many years these two men had engaged in ritualistic disavowals of one another because that was what their respective tribes wanted to hear. The process by which we travelled from there to where we ended up did not happen by chance, nor was it some maudlin reconciliation conducted for the sake of peace. It was a profound human interaction which collapsed the ideological, historical and political barriers between two men who happened to be politicians, because such a collapsing had first been achieved at a more general level. This one-on-one human reconciliation drew its energy from a profound change in the surrounding culture, and in turn nurtured the changes that had given it life.

The peace process was not something that happened on television, but, long before that, in the hearts and minds of the people. There had to be a process of thawing, initiated by the leaderships, but incapable of being dictated or contrived. Around the talks table, a formal method was called for: an engagement of moderates, followed by engagement of extremists. This too was a layer of the drama, vital to the unfolding of the deeper one.

But this was still just the formal political process, depending for its viability on a deeper process in the imagination of society, and, beneath this collective imagination, in the individual heart of every member of that society, contriving to change him- or herself in ways that cannot be measured or discounted. Ultimately, it was not the politicians who changed Ireland, but the people, one by one, in our private hearts, allowing our deepest antagonisms and prejudices to melt away in the hope of a brighter dawn.

And yet the story can only be told, comprehended, as a drama in which the King of the Culture, flawed and flamboyant, was Ian Paisley. And here was the deeper truth about Paisley: that, despite his protestations, he was at least as Irish as anyone else and more so than most of those who claimed the condition. For who, beholding the extravagant dimensions of his remarkable personality, could conclude other than that he emerged from the mists of some Celtic identity crisis? In truth, he was as 'British' as the Pope of Rome.

And this is perhaps the tragedy of Ireland in summary: that neither part of itself could recognize itself even in this, its most vibrant and passionate manifestation. For if, four decades earlier, we could have got to know each other as well as we got to know each other in the end, the whole sorry bother could have been substituted with a brief but hearty slanging match.

31 Martin Cahill

Around the end of the 1980s, an odd figure emerged into the grey light of an Ireland still struggling with recession. His name was Martin Cahill, but he called himself 'The General', and he was, by all accounts, a major criminal and a thoroughly nasty piece of work. But then, almost overnight, he became something of a star.

First he appeared on the primetime television current affairs programme, *Today Tonight*, wearing an anorak with the hood pulled up and with his hand covering his face. Sometimes he wore Mickey Mouse T-shirts and once he dropped his pants to show he was wearing Mickey Mouse shorts. Emerging from a period in Garda custody, he would wear a homemade balaclava and, as he made his way through the throng of reporters, hum to himself a simple tune.

Cahill was rumoured to have an unusual domestic arrangement: he was living simultaneously with two sisters, in two different houses. He came across as great crack altogether. He had an easy line in humour and some great yarns about how he would take the mickey (Mickey Mouse, geddit?) out of the cops who were keeping him under constant surveillance. Nobody was quite clear what this surveillance was intended to achieve, since Cahill was unlikely to try to commit any crime while he was being watched.

Nodding satirically towards his garda escort, The General would inform journalists that he was thinking of advertising for an armed garda escort for the movement of large amounts of cash. It would have been easy to forget that this joker had once nailed a criminal 'colleague' to the floor.

Cahill had spent most of his adult life in jail, mainly for relatively trivial offences. He had been suspected of many crimes, including the 1986 robbery of eleven priceless paintings in the Beit collection from Russborough House, County Wicklow. The haul included a Vermeer, a Goya and a Rubens.

Cahill had immense respect for An Garda Síochána. He believed it was a mistake to underestimate them, and the lengths to which they might go in order to get their man. Still, he regarded his dealings with them as a game, in which the main thing was not to show a reaction. In prison he learned to read, and read Dale Carnegie's book, *How to Win Friends and Influence People*.

Martin Cahill told of an impoverished childhood. He had grown up as one of 12 children, the son of a lighthouse keeper. Convicted of his first criminal offence even before he entered his teens, he had spent time in Daingean reformatory, one of the most notorious of those Church-run institutions for orphans and wayward children which would in 2009 be exposed in the Ryan Report into abuse in Catholic-run institutions. When he was released from Daingean, he remained at liberty for two years before being jailed for four years for handling stolen property.

The General was to change not merely the popular concept of criminality in Ireland but also the way crime was reported. He would become the first subject of a new style of crime reporting, in which a kind of irony entered into what had previously been an unambiguously serious business. Thenceforth, the most gruesome thugs and sadists were given nicknames and written about as though they were soap stars, which in a sense they now were. Cahill was the first of a new breed of allegedly lovable criminals, the old rogue with a heart of gold who saw himself as a modern-day Robin Hood. He spoke about his deprived childhood and seemed to take it for granted that this justified his grown-up activities.

The Robin Hood subtext began to enter into the reporting of nearly all criminality. No story of the evil deeds of the latest drug warlord was complete without an account of his impoverished childhood and grievances against 'the system'. Before The General, crimes were reported as offences against society, simple breaches of the law, demanding detection and punishment. But, after him, every criminal became potential inspiration for a film, or a novel, in which the 'backstory' was invariably rooted in a troubled past and a desire to 'get even' with society.

A new breed of crime reporter emerged who became to the criminal underworld what gossip writers had been to the showbiz scene. They wrote about the private lives of criminals, their sex lives, their rumoured deeds, heroic and otherwise. The reporters featured in dramatic television ads and created the impression that all this had something to do with investigative journalism. The criminal underworld, flattered by the attention, began to compete for stardom.

And this development seemed to be related to an even more ominous syndrome. Invariably in the wake of criminal outrages, the voices of certain journalists and amateur sociologists were to be heard even above the grief of those left bereaved by the actions of some monstrous Robin Hood. Eschewing the obvious explanation that the perpetrators of such obscenities were simply irredeemably evil, these voices speak of 'alienation' and 'context', explaining that such things happen because the perpetrators come from a class in society disenfranchised by virtue of economic and social marginalization.

As the years wore on, the crime figures went through the roof. Gang warfare broke out in several Irish cities, most notably Limerick. The media were hard-pressed to keep coming up with original nicknames for the criminals who came and often, despatched by the next in line for stardom, went.

Although the social theoreticians prated about social deprivation, the evidence was to the contrary. In the 20 years after Martin Cahill made his first television appearance, most sections of Irish society became steadily wealthier. It is true that an imbecilic social policy, which pursued unchecked urbanization as a path to 'modernity' and 'progress', had created appalling social ghettoes in many cities and towns, and that, as a consequence of short-sighted social welfare policies, these had become festering cesspits of idleness, ignorance, brutishness and self-destruction. But the deeper, cultural change was that, in tandem with the growth of these jungles there had evolved a stream of public thought that sought to play down the imperative of personal responsibility in deciding that all wrongdoing emanating from these ghettoes could be explained by reference to 'social factors'. Following an initial bout of public horror in the wake of each new outrage, the voices of enlightenment reasserted themselves to speak of 'marginalization' and 'alienation', thus destroying any chance of a concerted initiative against thuggery.

There is something to be said for the 'social context' analysis of crime – provided it is advanced purely as a cautionary note concerning the implications of social policy. Undoubtedly, the vast majority of the Irish criminal classes tend to emanate from the social welfare jungles we have deposited on the edges of our cities and towns. But to observe this as evidence of social policy mistakes is quite a different thing to advancing it in exculpation of criminal and murderous behaviour.

There is evidence that, since the brief stardom of Martin Cahill, self-justification on the basis of 'social deprivation' is becoming increasingly fashionable among criminals when they are apprehended. Even more worrying is the tendency for such notions to be trotted out by judges sitting in cases where these issues are highly irrelevant. One eminent judge, sentencing in a manslaughter case, made much of his negative impressions on a visit to the area where the convicted individual had grown up, making it clear that he was handing down a reduced sentence on this account. Martin Cahill, had he still been around, would have approved. He had been shot dead one August 1994 afternoon in the street, allegedly by the IRA in one of its final pre-ceasefire clean-up operations.

32 Sean Doherty

When Sean Doherty came to prominence in Irish politics in the early 1980s, Ireland had been in the throes of a culture war for more than a decade. Though centred on the personality of Charles Haughey, this war drew its energy from the struggle to change Ireland from what it had been to what it 'should' be. It was bound up with the 'national question', but more fundamentally with the tension between practitioners of the old-style, pejoratively termed 'clientelist' model of politics, that is Haughey and Doherty, and a modernizing tendency which demanded that we abandon the parish-pump and embrace the new, technocratic model which required politicians to be legislators first and public representatives as an afterthought. At issue was the very nature of Ireland and the drafting of a commonly agreed version of the kind of society we should become.

The key moral questions related not so much to right and wrong, as to 'Which side are you on?' All this tension and drama was perhaps inevitable in a society which had lately moved from domination and dependency to its first baby steps of political and economic independence. The struggle that occurred in Sean Doherty's time was really between, on the one hand, those who through fate and circumstances had garnered the resources to escape the implications of the past and, on the other, those who had been left behind to make

their own way. The former demanded a new, shiny, exemplary modernity, while the latter perceived themselves as still enwrapped in a history they could not so easily brush aside.

The main reason it has become difficult to argue with those who continued to pour scorn on Doherty and Haughey for both outlook and deed was not because the moral perspective of such detractors was irrefutable. It was also because *they* had won the war and so succeeded in imposing their version of events and morality on the public realm and consciousness.

The most notorious of Doherty's actions was his ordering, as Minister for Justice, of garda taps on the phones of two political journalists at the height of the leadership struggles that convulsed Fianna Fáil in government in the early 1980s. Doherty, like other ministers at the time, was concerned about leaks from the cabinet table, suspecting Haughey's main longtime rival, George Colley. In tapping the phones of two journalists, however, he stepped outside the party political arena and embroiled senior garda officers in what was undoubtedly an illegal, as well as wholly bizarre, burst of activity. Sean Doherty's claim – that he ordered the tapping of the telephones of Bruce Arnold and Geraldine Kennedy on the basis that cabinet confidentiality was being breached, and he wanted to discover who was breaching it – is easily dismissed as self-serving in the culture created for, and by, the winners. And it is literally impossible to argue with this verdict because Doherty ended up on the losing side.

A lot of the indignation about Doherty, and the demonization arising from it, was simply a conflation of events into a particular set of meanings, which were, above all, convenient. This doesn't necessarily mean that the tapping of the phones of two senior political journalists was legally correct or otherwise justifiable, but for some people, including Sean Doherty, it was possible to justify from where they sat.

To even try to explain Doherty's actions or personality in the language and logic of the re-created culture is inevitably to attract accusations of defending the indefensible. But the justifications he offered for his actions were arguably valid when you see things from where he, and his followers and supporters, saw them.

Thus, the series of 'grotesque, unbelievable, bizarre and unprecedented' events that became known as GUBU and defined the early 1980s era of Haughey's leadership, came down to questions of perspective, which in turn depended on which side you were on. When Haughey and Doherty were on the same side, they were equally derided by the modernizing tendency, which repudiated as embarrassments residual elements of what they regarded as an outmoded Ireland. Haughey came to embody all of their prejudices, not because he was of the culture that was so despised (he was but had left it far behind) but because, in seeking to rebuild his own political reputation after the Arms Trial, he had appealed successfully to this constituency and had secured his rehabilitated persona on a rhetorical genuflection in its direction.

In the 1980s, however, a strange thing happened. Haughey had been banished after GUBU and spent four years in opposition. Only the dire state of the economy and the abject failure of the Fine Gael/Labour coalition to deal with the emergency gave him a second chance. The reluctant consensus among media commentators and economists was that Haughey might make a better fist of running the economy, and GUBU was, as far as it concerned Haughey at least, airbrushed out of the picture.

It would be more accurate, however, to say that the ghosts of GUBU had been temporarily exorcized from the persona of Charles Haughey and transferred to the enigmatic persona of Sean Doherty. It has been interesting to observe that, whatever negativities Haughey and Doherty together represented were in some sense perceived to be more acute in Doherty than they had ever been in Haughey. But there is also the fascinating possibility that the anger of those who opposed Haughey was never really personal against him – what they mainly hated was that he had 'chosen' the 'ordinary' people of Ireland over them. Later, when division opened up between Doherty and Haughey, some of Haughey's most celebrated media detractors bizarrely rushed to defend him, at least to the extent of kicking more determinedly his former friend.

And Haughey even briefly tried to exploit this tendency by playing to the fact that the prejudices of his own enemies were even more strongly pitted against Doherty than against himself. There was a remarkable moment in the press conference Haughey held in January 1992 to respond to the allegations of Sean Doherty that he, Doherty, had told Haughey about the tapping of the two journalists' phones and had given him transcripts of the taps. Asked by one journalist if he thought Doherty's initiative was related to the leadership bid of Albert Reynolds 'and the so-called Western alliance', Haughey threw back his head, laughed and corrected him: 'You mean the *country* and western alliance!' For a moment, the hostility of the press conference dissipated and Haughey had most of the journalists again laughing and eating out of his hand. This pandering to the smug prejudices of supposed sophisticates whose self-confidence went no further than a snobbish sense of superiority based on living in a street rather than a field was the moment when Charles Haughey betrayed the very people he had courted to become Fianna Fáil leader and Taoiseach.

There are some senses in which Sean Doherty was to blame for much of what happened to him. He was a scapegoat, but never quite a victim. He had a perverse streak in his character which caused him to play up to the role allotted to him by his enemies. He was so full of mischief and such a convincing actor that there were times when he seemed to be relishing the notion of himself as this crazed lynch-lawman, standing in judgement on his adversaries by virtue of his office. Part of the trouble was that the media presentation of Doherty as some kind of tribal backwoodsman led his enormous intelligence to be totally underestimated, and this meant that nobody quite gave him credit for the irony he exuded much of the time

How seriously you regarded any of it depended on where you stood, which side of the tracks you came from. The telephone tapping incident was either an outrageous abuse of office for party political purposes or an entirely justifiable attempt to protect the Taoiseach of the day from the subversive energies of his internal enemies. Perhaps, in the end, Doherty's real mistake was in tapping the phones of Arnold and Kennedy, when he should have been tapping George Colley's.

33 Tony Blair

Because Tony Blair's mother came from Ireland, he is, strictly speaking, 'half-Irish'. Had he, for example, been possessed of football skills at approximately the level of his apparent gift for politics, he might well have made it on to the Irish football team, perhaps ending up as captain. But Blair's contribution to Irish politics is at a deeper level than anything to do with blood or nationhood. For a decade he came among us, persuaded us that all things were possible, and then went away, leaving us bereft.

Blair's trick was his deceptive ordinariness, which was actually not a deception. To begin with, he had no talent for politics. Sensibly, he wanted to be a rock star, but he failed to make the grade in that calling, and discovered that politics was easier than it looked and that almost none of those involved in it were particularly good at it. He latched on to Gordon Brown, stole all his best ideas and then wiped his eye.

Most British people have no idea how much we Irish know about them, having watched them and absorbed their popular culture all our lives. *Top of the Pops*, *Bunty*, Shakespeare, Enid Blyton, John Peel, Man. U., Agatha Christie, *The Hotspur*, Whispering Bob Harris – all these are as much part of Irish culture as British. Out of politeness, we invariably acquiesce in their attitude of superiority, but in truth we know everything about them, whereas they know almost nothing about us except U2 and the IRA.

But we, for our part, and for perhaps understandable historical reasons, tend to overlook the profound impact our neighbours' politics has on ours. Almost unconsciously, we follow trends set 'across the water', not so much in the realm of ideas and -isms as in the demeanour of the political animal. We had no equivalent of Thatcher, but nevertheless, from the mid-1980s, Irish politics took on something of her certitude. Charles Haughey (certainly no fan of the Iron Lady), adopted something of her thinking in addressing the mess that he had contributed to making of the Irish economy. We called it 'monetarism', a misuse of the term which for years used to drive Irish economists mad.

In the Tiger years, our aesthetic of leadership gathered what it had of inspiration almost entirely from Blair: the matey affability of Bertie and Enda seeming to arise from an unconscious desire to emulate Blair's successful reworking of the Kennedy brand.

Blair was actually one smart bastard. Politics seemed easy to him not because he was particularly suited to it, but because it had become so predictable and banal. When he turned his attention to the situation in the north of Ireland, for example, the first thing that occurred to him was how stupid it was that nobody had ever been able to sort it out. For him it was simply a matter of flattering a few hick politicians and getting them to feel superior to one another. Within a year of moving into 10 Downing Street, he had engineered the Good Friday Agreement.

The resolution of the conflict was in large part due to the fact that a generation of men who had wasted their lives in this futile war were now prepared to act to stop the disease being passed on to their children. But the magic ingredient was Tony Blair. A born-again 1960s idealist disguised as spin doctor's puppet, he was able to alter mindsets without frightening the horses with piety, ideology or historical baggage.

The veteran socialist Leo Abse, who later wrote a book about Blair, said that he had an innate desire to place everything in a conflict-free zone. His first instinct was his desire to anticipate objections and to appease objectors even before they spoke. His essential view of life was that all evidence of differences should be minimized. For Abse this was a defect of Blair's but for us in Ireland, as perhaps for nobody else, these values paid off. Because of his unique psychology, Tony Blair made things happen that otherwise would not have happened.

But the only thing more banal than politics is the culture of the commentary that largely attends it, and this has grown exponentially worse in recent years because of contamination by what is sometimes called 'citizen journalism'. When the bloggers and their literal-minded equivalents in the 'old' media were not spitting at Blair because of his role in the invasion of Iraq, they were dismissing him as the sultan of spin. But although he was undoubtedly a skilful politician of the media age, Blair also exhibited a deep seriousness which counterpointed his superstar image. You only have to look dispassionately at his record to know that here was a politician who used his accidental bounty of charisma to conceal a deeply serious heart, in many ways out of tempo with its time. Blair seemed instinctively to know what was necessary for survival in an age in which charismatic vacuity was prized over everything, and to guard his deeper thoughts and talents until he was able to put them to what he regarded as their proper use – even if this was to lead to an almost terminal unpopularity.

As his period of leadership rolled out, the clichés about Blair were that he was cunning and ruthless; that he was consumed with presentation over substance, that he was not 'real', but the product of the spells of unelected spin doctors charged, above all, with getting his government re-elected. There is a name for this syndrome: 'politics'. Blair's personality and methodology were problematic only for those who had failed to reflect upon the change that has occurred in modern politics since the introduction of opinion polling, which had caused the thought process of politics to become like an air-con unit, endlessly recycling the same banal ideas and periodically re-presenting them in a new way.

For Blair, there was never an issue about whether or not he should concentrate on image and presentation, only about whether he could become sufficiently adept at these dark arts to win. Pandering to 'public opinion' was, as he immediately intuited, the name of the game. Once elected, the issue was not whether he would, could or should engage in the politics of perception, but whether he could do so and manage to achieve anything worthwhile in spite of the culture of the sample poll, that elusive unit of public opinion which all modern political parties must struggle to decipher and understand.

What is interpreted as 'public opinion' from these surveys is not the perspective of real people, but the cybernetic response of quota-controlled samples. These deliver not so much a reflection of the views of society as of the debased unit of public opinion created by a circular process involving pseudo-moralistic hectoring on the part of the media, choreographed posturing on the part of politicians, and political correctness on the part of the polled public, resulting in a currency that is further debased with each cycle of the machine. This means that it is necessary for the modern politician to speak at all times with forked tongue: simultaneously in the language of idealism to those who make things happen in the economy and society, and in the languages of piety and sentimentality for the benefit of statistics. The challenge is maintaining the correct balance between these conflicting imperatives to allow important things to be done while still holding the stage.

The problem for the political culture he left behind is that Blair was an outsider in politics, whom the insiders immediately started to imitate. By succeeding in the ways he did, he bequeathed us an entire generation of Blair clones from within that stupid, hopeless world, who think they can achieve all the good things he did while avoiding all the pitfalls.

In the UK, David Cameron and Nick Clegg thought they could fill his shoes by wearing the right suit and a smile. In Ireland, Bertie Ahern managed to bask and share in the Blair magic for a decade while maintaining something of his own identity. Then, George Lee became so intoxicated with what you could do with a suit and a smile that he briefly gave up his good job in RTE in an attempt to save the nation.

Next, the Irish people watched in apprehension as Simon Coveny and Leo Varadkar warmed up in the wings.

What they all missed about Blair was that he wasn't really a politician at all. He was a superior intelligence, a Man from Mars who decided to play at being a politician because he could see how stupid and hopeless it all was and how easy it might be to achieve things if you just applied common sense and reason to processes usually governed by tribalism, sanctimony and pretence. Unfortunately, his imitators, who have the suits and the smiles but not the sense or the smarts, will be with us verily unto the end of time.

34 Charlie Bird

In the months and then, God help us, years after the flight of the Celtic Tiger, the media became the highest court in the land. With politicians determined to take the 'respectable' option at all costs, and, ultimately, to require the citizen to carry the can, it soon became clear that there was no real possibility that many of those who had pauperized the country would be brought to anything resembling justice. The important thing, from the politicians' perspective, was getting everything up and running again. Sure, a couple of retired bankers could be thrown to the pack, but it remained a refrain of governmental rhetoric that the survival of the banking system was essential to a revival of national fortunes. For this to work, the government needed to direct public anger towards a handful of targets that were no longer central to the plans for reconstructing the banking system.

In this climate, the media became the Supreme Court of a kind of national desire to kick the miscreants in the shins. But, instead of pursuing politicians on why they were unprepared to pursue radical options, journalists went for the easy option of chasing scapegoats wearing their jackets on their heads. Those who sought to outline the cultural context to the crisis were sidelined as the frontline reporters pursued incidentals like pension top-ups for retiring banking executives. This fuelled public anger but also reduced its focus to the peripheral symptoms of the problem. In this environment, Charlie Bird became the Chief Prosecutor of Easy Targets.

If there was a retired banker or a failed developer to be pursued, Charlie was your man. There was no hiding place. Charlie, in his resumed capacity as RTE's Very Important Big Chief Head of No Ordinary Reporting, would tiptoe to the wrongdoer's door, whisperingly confiding to viewers his intention to ask some serious questions. He would knock and wait. The viewer would be enabled to observe a Mercedes in the driveway, or any sign of Georgian splendour about the residence. Silence would ensue. Charlie would knock again. A voice inside might say, 'Go away', or words to that effect, or 'I have nothing to say'. Charlie would hold his ground. 'What about such 'n' such?', he would demand through the letterbox. 'What about the missing money, Mr So 'n' So?' 'I have nothing to say', Mr So 'n' so would say.

On, perhaps appropriately, 1 April 2010, Charlie Bird, in his capacity as RTE Chief of All Washington Correspondents, sought to doorstep the former Anglo Irish Chief Executive David Drumm at his $4.5 million home in Cape Cod, Massachusetts.

As our hero made his way up the driveway, Charlie's voiceover set the scene; 'As we approached the house, it had all the appearance as if there was no one at home.'

He reached the front door and looked through the glass.

'Oh, he's there,' Charlie exclaimed to no one in particular. 'They're there!'

A voice could be heard shouting indistinctly from inside.

'Mr Drumm. It's Charlie Bird from RTE.'

The Voice again.

'Why are you ducking down?' Charlie continued.

The Voice said something about whether Charlie had seen what it said on the gate.

Charlie became just a little irate. His voice went up an octave, which made him sound peevish. 'I WANT TO TALK TO YOU,' he said.

The voice said something about its family being there.

'Well,' said Charlie, 'can I talk to you outside?'

The Voice seemed to say no.

'There are taxpayers at home in Ireland who would like some answers,' said Charlie, now fully into his stride.

The Voice was having none of it.

Charlie started again and then thought better of it. 'There's some taxpayers . . . Okay. Thank you very much.'

This was regarded as the height of journalistic endeavour. Charlie Bird, long a hero of the Irish public, again became the object of widespread gratitude and respect. 'At least we have Charlie Bird,' people would reflect, 'to ask the hard questions.'

It has often been observed that the first response of most Irish people to the mention of Charlie Bird is a broad smile. It is a smile containing elements of condescension and amusement, but also of intense affection. In the massive cultural changes that have swept through Irish life in recent decades, Charlie Bird has become a kind of avenging angel. To emphasize his importance to Irish life, his title has been extended, making it longer and more important-sounding with every passing year. First he was a mere Reporter; then he became a Correspondent; then a Special Correspondent, then a Chief Special Correspondent.

There was a time when tax evasion and white-collar crime were part of the fabric of Irish life, the subject of discreet nods and winks, indulgent smiles and shaking of heads. Nowadays they are regarded, at the level of public conversation at least, much in the way a parish priest might once have regarded the phenomenon of auto-eroticism. Charlie Bird has become the national chronicler of previously unspoken sins. His postbag has for years been by far the largest of any RTE news and current affairs reporter, presumably divided between outraged citizens selling out their neighbours for tax evasion and contrite wrongdoers unburdening themselves of their own sins. His is the voice of the national conscience, the facilitator of the collective confession. When a scandal breaks in the corridors of power or high finance, it is Charlie who guides the wrongdoer towards a tearful blurt of remorse, though always on camera, with Charlie standing by to express the hurt and incomprehension of the man in the street. 'But do you not think,' he might probe, 'that you owe the Irish people an explanation?' 'Mr So 'n' So,' he would earnestly demand, 'do you accept that what you've done is very, very wrong?'

The Irish people are delighted with all this. Most of them would have been shocked to discover that Charlie Bird was once a militant left-winger, and that he was photographed at the graveside of a dead comrade giving a clenched fist salute alongside the notorious left-wing agitator Tariq Ali. Nowadays Charlie gives few hints of such a colourful past.

His full name is Charles Brown Bird, although he spent a brief period in the 1960s as Cathal Mac an Ein, and another as Cathal Mac Einigh after someone pointed out that 'Son of the Bird' was a daft name for a serious reporter. The 'Brown' part derived from the fact that, on emerging from his mother's womb, Charlie was a deep brown, the consequence of the iodine tablets taken for a thyroid condition Mother Bird had developed during pregnancy. Another brother was named 'Dickie'.

Perhaps this initial colouring was by way of a prophecy concerning Charlie's future role as the National Pursuer of Brown Envelopes. For three decades, Bird has been the People's Witness to disaster. Following Hurricane Charlie in the 1980s, he took to the street in a gondola. In one memorable sequence, he approached a man who was sitting on the roof of his house, with the water lapping at the gutters. Before Charlie could speak, the man declared, 'You're too late, Charlie. Go away or I'll put your head under the water!'

One time, when he was Taoiseach, Charles Haughey, a keen sportsman, sent his Christian-namesake a brace of duck as a gesture of admiration. Bird, however, saw it as a Mafia-style warning. Although personally a gracious and charming individual, in his public demeanour he comes across as humourless and even priggish. Charlie seems to embody some deep, brooding piety in the national imagination that, while buried deep under cute-hoorism and 'the Crack', emerges every so often to launch literalized, projected accusations at anyone who happens to get caught.

Charlie Bird undertakes journalism as though every day is a movie. He is, as one journalist memorably put it, 'a Lois Lane who shaves'. His nightly pantomimes have added greatly to the gaiety of the nation and made him into a national figure. But the question must be asked: does knocking on front doors and demanding that bankers submit themselves to interrogation by Charlie really achieve anything beyond creating diversion and entertainment for the viewers of the nine o'clock news? The Charlie Bird brand of slapstick investigation probably attracts far more viewers than a thorough, and tedious, exposition and analysis of the facts, and in this sense it might be called more influential. But it also results in the consolidation of a national mindset whereby public rage and indignation is channelled into a kind of sadistic glee at the dis-comfiture of Charlie's latest 'subject', and then allowed to hiss harmlessly into the stratosphere.

35 Niall Crowley

A few years ago, one Philip Tobin, Managing Director of DotCom Directories, a Dublin-based e-commerce business, advertised some positions in his company with the proviso 'no smokers need apply'. After the ad first appeared in a freesheet newspaper, Mr Tobin received a call from someone at the Equality Authority who told him that his advert was against the law because it discriminated against smokers and he would have to withdraw it. Mr Tobin said that the ad had fulfilled its function and so the question of withdrawing it did not arise. It soon turned out that the Equality Authority was wrong – there was nothing in the legislation governing its operation to say that smokers cannot be discriminated against.

Nor, any sensible person would say, should there be. The Equality Authority was, after all, a state body. A couple of years before this, to the most tremendous fanfare, the government had introduced a ban on smoking in the workplace because smoking is bad for people's health. Yet, another branch of government saw fit to ring up a businessman who has come to the same conclusion to accuse him of breaking the law.

The Equality Authority sat down with itself and had a rethink. It then issued a statement explaining that, in fact, there had been 'no question of discrimination'.

In fact, there had been a distinct question of discrimination. Mr Tobin had been on every radio programme in the state for the previous week telling the nation how much he disliked smoking and what he thought of smokers. He said they were smelly, stupid, unhealthy time-wasters, and he did not want them working for him.

We are nowadays so accustomed to certain types of people complaining they've been discriminated against that we think there's something wrong with discrimination *per se*. But we discriminate all the time, between shops or places we like to go to and those we don't, between radio stations and newspapers we like or don't like to read and listen to, between columnists we read and those we don't. We also discriminate between people we like to mix with and people we don't, people we trust and people we don't, people we like the look of and people we don't.

The idea that the Equality Authority exists to eliminate discrimination is a myth. In fact, it exists to enforce certain forms of discrimination. In this case, the Equality Authority representative who initially contacted Mr Tobin was seeking to compel him to discriminate in favour of smokers, even though he dislikes smoking and thinks smokers would be bad for his business. If the logic of this contact had held sway, we would be but a hairsbreadth away from affirmative action in favour of smokers, and legal requirements that employers hire minimum numbers of nicotine addicts. This sounds daft, but it is no more so than most of what the Equality Authority spends its time doing.

'Equality' in this sense, of course, does not mean what it says in the dictionary. 'Equality', as bandied about in latter-day public conversation, is really a concept concerned with acquiring for certain listed categories the rights, entitlements and privileges deemed, by definition, to have been unjustly acquired by others. It is, in other words, a rebalancing process, in an equation deemed by the guiding ideology to have an unjust and immoral configuration as it stands. Thus, there must be a rebalancing between men and women in favour of women, blacks and whites in favour of blacks, homosexuals and heterosexuals in favour of homosexuals, and so forth. There is not, however, any requirement that the exchange work both ways. Men must yield to women on whatever grounds are ordained by the relevant authorities, but there is no question of women ceding anything to men, even where a case is made that the status quo is inequitable and unjust in a way that favours women.

Since its foundation in 2001, the CEO of the Equality Authority had been Niall Crowley. His tenure ensured that, right through the Noughties, the word 'equality', as politically defined in the public realm, became a construct that excluded men. Crowley's job was to target harmful discrimination, but instead he chose to impose a highly selective definition of the word 'equality' and, in effect, to conduct a war against one half of the population, allegedly on behalf of the other half.

Here is a direct quote from a speech Crowley made while CEO of the Equality Authority: 'The primary objective for work on men in gender equality must be to strengthen the role and contribution of men in challenging and changing the structures, institutional policies and practices, and culture (including stereotypical attitudes), that generate and sustain the inequalities experienced by women.' Translation: everyone is entitled to equality, but men are entitled only to 'share' in the 'equality' of women. Crowley emerged from an ideological heartland in which the word 'equality' to been redefined to make it the exclusive preserve of certain listed groups. In his role in the Equality Authority, he went to court to have women made full members of elite golf clubs, and lost significant amounts of taxpayers' money when the authority's case was shot down. Under his stewardship the authority was enthusiastically supportive of a demand for adoption rights for gay couples, the right of travellers to become an officially recognized ethnic group, and the right of women to demand a share in everything men were presumed to have without giving up anything. But it seemed to regard itself as having no role in relation to men *as men*, or to have nothing to say about the injustices men might be suffering by virtue of not belonging to a named victim group.

The attitude of the 'equality' lobby to gay adoption rights is especially instructive. For here is a context in which there exists a clear conflict between what are self-evidently the natural rights of two groups – fathers and children – and another, gays. The 'equality' lobby rushed to support not those whose natural rights were being trampled into the dust of history but those who claimed an entitlement not on the basis of reason or nature, but on their status as a favoured 'listed category'.

Crowley claimed to have addressed himself to changing structures and systems so as to create 'a better society for women and men'. This would have been laudable, but he did not do it. Instead, he addressed only those structures and systems that corresponded to his ideological prejudices. The rest he ignored, which means that many, many men, and many of these men's children, were infinitely unhappier at the end of his term of office than might otherwise have been the case. Like a piano tuner who tuned only the white keys and refused to touch or listen to the black notes, he left the instrument as out of tune as it ever was, only in a different way.

36 Terry Keane

In the opening chapter of *The Begrudger's Guide to Irish Politics*, Breandán Ó hEithir quoted a doughty Cork blacksmith, on the day after the signing of the Anglo-Irish Treaty in 1921, responding to his parish priest's assurance that 'We're going to have our own gentry now', with a spirited 'We will in our arse have our own gentry'.

The Keane Edge was perhaps independent Ireland's most determined effort to prove him wrong. Through the early years of the Celtic Tiger, this gossip column on the back of the lifestyle section of the *Sunday Independent*, with its snippets about the rich and famous, sought to insinuate a new social hierarchy in a nation no longer sure where it should draw its values from. Judging by the Keane Edge, money, glamour, celebrity and brass neck became the most visible characteristics of social significance in this new Ireland.

Terry Keane, because she was 'known' to be conducting a long-term affair with Charles Haughey, was the perfect frontperson for this showcase of Ireland's emerging 'gentry'. The facts of this affair were 'known' in much the way people 'know' about such things in small towns – it was common currency without ever being openly stated. It was hinted at, then denied, again let slip and again with-drawn. Terry Keane was the wife of a man who had been appointed a senior judge by Haughey himself. It was all too fantastic for an Ireland raised on the Catechism to grapple with.

In the 1990s, this became a meal ticket for Terry Keane, after she moved from the *Sunday Press*, where she had been a lightweight feature writer, to become a high-profile gossip columnist with the *Sunday Independent*. The persistent innuendos about Haughey gave her a cachet nobody else could touch, and she was, by all accounts, paid as much for this connection as for any writing talent she possessed.

Keane's relationship with Haughey became the subject of persistent references and innuendos in the Keane Edge. There would be mentions of weekends in Paris with this unnamed 'Sweetie', or allusions, so barefaced as to seem implausible in their obvious implication, to 'my Charlie'. It was all exceedingly arch and therefore both titillating and deniable.

In May 1999, Terry Keane moved from the *Sunday Independent* to the *Sunday Times* in a deal which involved her writing three initial articles about her long-time romantic relationship with Charles Haughey and thereafter a gossip column for two years. She received £65,000 for the three initial articles and £50,000 per annum for the next two years. These three articles, based on her putative forthcoming memoirs, were published on three successive Sundays that May.

In advance of publication of the first instalment, Keane went on *The Late Late Show*, for the penultimate show of Gay Byrne's lengthy tenure, and spilled the beans on her relationship with CJH.

In a fourth, apparently unscheduled piece on 6 June, Keane responded to critics and dealt with the history of her infamous *Sunday Independent* column. She had left the *Sunday Independent* without notice and there was now clearly bad blood between herself and editor Aengus Fanning and his deputy editor Anne Harris. Fanning had been quoted in his own newspaper as saying 'She was happy to take our money while making no contribution. Her work rate had declined dramatically in the last two years.' Gradually it emerged that Keane had just been one of a team of journalists contributing to the column that bore her name.

The *Sunday Times'* front page lead that morning was entitled 'Bono story my worst mistake says Terry Keane'. This referred to a notorious Keane Edge story which revealed the sex of one of Bono's children on the basis of information leaked from the maternity hospital before Bono himself had been told. In this interview, Keane apologized for the episode, describing it as 'the most indefensible thing I ever did'.

'I was not aware of the story before it was published and when I saw it I was shocked. I should have resigned there and then. It was my worst mistake and my bitterest regret.'

She described the Keane Edge column as 'poisonous', claiming it had been mostly written by other people under the guidance of Anne Harris. Harris, she said, was 'undoubtedly the cleverest woman I have met. She knew exactly what the readership wanted and however much people used to berate the column, there was no doubt they read it and the circulation soared. I just wish she had used her own name and not mine.

'The Keane Edge gave the impression that I was the sole author, but at any one time, a minimum of five people worked on the column, usually six or seven.

'There is just one burning regret in my fifty-nine years – the hurt and damage I caused to people through the Keane Edge . . . I should have stopped sooner and walked away. Quite simply, I needed the money. Despite the apparent glamour of my life, I have always been financially insecure.

'At the beginning, even though it was written in a very bitchy style, the Keane Edge was not intrusive. Gradually it changed direction. I was partly responsible for that and therefore I take part of the blame. Part, but not all.

'When it started to go too far and I became uncomfortable with it, I was always assured by my superiors that the readers knew the Terry Keane of the Keane Edge was a fantasy character, not the real me. I could see their point. I doubt that readers took it at face value that I was constantly on the phone to Warren Beatty and Brad Pitt, and that I was the world's most stunning and irresistible redhead sex bomb. So reassured, my disquiet would evaporate.'

In the same edition, the *Sunday Times* carried an interview with Terry Keane by another *ST* journalist, which claimed that Keane had been devastated by the hostile responses to her *Sunday Times* revelations. 'It has been like having one's eyeballs sliced through with razor blades. But this too shall pass.'

Asked how she could have been unaware of the pain and damage inflicted by the Keane Edge, she replied: 'It seems to me that I must have been living in a different world. The vehemence with which people react to the Keane Edge . . . shocks me. The fact that I'm unaware of that revulsion means either that I am very dim or completely amoral. That frightens me, as I don't think I'm dim.'

In a way, the Keane Edge was like a cultural weathervane, rendering visible the implicit facts of the Celtic Tiger years. Nothing about it, not even the identity of its author, was authentic, and it therefore, in retrospect, acquired the status of metaphor. It was something the Irish public was drawn to, and while they laughed at much of what it contained, they envied, too, the lifestyles depicted there. It invested them with a kind of idealism that fed, in turn, the lesser desires of more humble ambitions. In this, it became a central element of the delusion that enveloped the country in those years. Terry Keane may not have written much of it, but her persona was certainly the grit around which this pearl of pretension and vanity was formed. Her life and personality came to represent, in those years, the idea of classiness, chutzpah and style. Like many things about that Ireland, the Keane Edge was not the product of one mind, nor even of all the minds that contributed to it. In a way, it was the product of an entire society running away with itself, of readers as much as journalists, wannabe celebrities and publicity seekers. And it seemed, in the end, entirely appropriate that the woman named as the author was 'only doing it for the money'.

37 Frank Dunlop

In the early summer of 2009, Frank Dunlop was sent down for eighteen months on a charge of corruption. As a former government press secretary, the culmination of Dunlop's long-chronicled downfall was a big story. As usual in such circumstances, his incarceration was attended by a spate of vindictive and gloating newspaper headlines, including references to his being taken away handcuffed in a prison van, rather than in the 'top of the range Mercedes' in which he had arrived for the sentencing hearing. In a country once famed for its Christian compassion, anything to do with money or politics has recently begun to attract the kind of venom and unpleasantness previously reserved for crimes like paedophilia and premeditated murder.

Dunlop's crimes were serious and inexcusable. He was also, to be frank, not the most likeable of men, being burdened with a personality characterized by smugness, superciliousness and an intellectual arrogance without visible means of support. When he first appeared before the Flood planning tribunal, these characteristics were abundantly observable. But, after some initial resistance, Dunlop had begun singing like a nightingale. The nation watched him fade away to a shadow of his former self and saw in his eyes the look of humiliation and disgrace. And yet it was noticeable that he did not hide away, nor seek to justify his behaviour. He stood his ground, told his story and accepted his medicine without complaint. He went on working, writing books and studying for a law degree. He faced the music and still held his head high. Dunlop accepted his wrongdoing yet retained his essential dignity as a human being.

Yet, there were those who continued to believe that Dunlop was being highly selective in his musical repertoire, which may have gone some way to explaining the vindictiveness that greeted his incarceration.

Sentencing Dunlop, Judge Frank O'Donnell said the public interest required a custodial sentence, not just a rap on the knuckles. 'The word must go out from this court that the corruption of politicians, or anyone in public life, must attract significant penalties,' he told Dunlop. He said that, although there was no readily identifiable victim in this case, Dunlop had actively undermined the confidence of the public in the democratic system and had been motivated by gain.

Dunlop was by now clearly not a well man. He was into his 60s, his life-expectancy radically foreshortened by recent experiences. Contrary to what the judge implied in sentencing, Dunlop had already been grievously punished for his sins. He had been humiliated and disgraced, albeit as a consequence of his own actions. He had, by all accounts, lost his friends. As a national figure, he had become the target of public rage and vindictiveness in a way 'ordinary' criminals do not.

Nobody could have suggested that Judge O'Donnell was a man lacking in compassion. Just a few days beforehand, he had suspended the entirety of a sentence of three years' imprisonment he handed down to a man who was before him on charges of robbing a pharmacy, apparently by demanding money with menaces. The man had twenty-three previous convictions, including a number of counts relating to drugs and robbery. Judge O'Donnell said it was a 'stupid' robbery, but accepted that all the cash had been recovered.

Judge O'Donnell pointed out that the charges against Frank Dunlop related to separate acts of corruption in 1992 and 1997, and noted that Dunlop had shown no hesitation in renewing his corrupt practices after a long gap. He had had every opportunity to reflect on what he was doing. The Judge added: 'Some people who come before me knowingly commit crimes through a haze of addiction. What you did, you did with a long-range, focused, criminal intent.'

It was an odd thing to interject, as though the Judge felt a need to justify himself. What possible connection could there be between Frank Dunlop and the kinds of people Judge O'Donnell was referring to? Indeed, it might be argued that Dunlop, too, was an addict: addicted, like so many of his countrymen, to money and power, and therefore perhaps just as worthy of compassion and mercy as an addict who endangered public safety in order to get his fix.

It is interesting how what is called justice often seems to follow the contours of public piety. Dunlop, with his not entirely attractive personality, made rather a good scapegoat. His jailing at this point went some little way towards appeasing a public seemingly insatiable in its need to see people walk the plank and climb the scaffold. Judge O'Donnell's words therefore caused a great outpouring of satisfaction in the land.

But the idea that Dunlop's incarceration would do anything to restore the public's faith in the planning process was a bit much. Planning in most parts of Ireland is opaque, arbitrary and shot through with a culture of ideological obstructionism. Anyone seeking to use the system soon discovers that it appears to be set up to create a context for people to find unorthodox ways around it. Or, perhaps you might say that it is set up to render necessary some extra-curricular assistance in finding ways around it. One planning authority in the west of the country, for example, requires members of the public who are seeking an appointment with a planner to call immediately after 9 a.m. on a Wednesday, in order to arrange an appointment for the following Monday week. All the available appointments are allocated within a few minutes, and, unless you can get through immediately after nine, you have no chance of getting to see a planner.

Most people seem to think this a normal way of doing business – whether through naïveté, righteousness or poverty, wearily and expensively trudging their way through the myriad of obstacles placed in the way of anyone seeking to get anything done. And when they were told to disapprove of 'corruption', most people did that as well, shaking their heads sadly at the criminality of Frank Dunlop and making no connection with their own experiences of bureaucracy and official obstructionism. And Frank, of course, duly obliged by looking the part of a once promising apparatchik gone to the bad. It did not seem to occur to anyone that it was perhaps the most natural thing in the world that businessmen in a hurry might see the need to pursue a different approach – that they might see the benefit of having a man with a brown envelope going around to grease the system's wheels a little. To suggest that this began or ended with Frank Dunlop was worthy of the constitution of Cloud Cuckoo Land. But somehow this was a lot easier than actually doing anything about it.

38 Charlie McCreevy

If they made movies about things as interesting as Irish politics, the story of Charles McCreevy might be among the more emblematic of the age: the Young Turk who blew the whistle on the greybeards who were sabotaging the economy, who was banished to the backbenches, then returned triumphant to become Minister for Finance in what would become the most successful period in his country's economic history.

In February 1982, Charlie McCreevy appeared on the cover of *Magill*, his face adorned by a headline which in its time did not read as overblown: 'Charlie McCreevy is Right. The Politicians Have Vandalized the Country.'

'Our politicians,' began Vincent Browne's article inside, 'have propelled us towards economic and social calamity in the last decade. Wild, irresponsible election promises and commitments, reckless public expenditure schemes, uncontrolled deficit budgeting and an unprecedented falsification of budget figures have coalesced to create the worst economic crisis the State has ever known. One politician has spoken out against this drift in national politics, Charlie McCreevy, and because he has done so outside the cosy confines of his party rooms he is being chastised.'

McCreevy, then a tender thirty-two-year-old, had been making his views on the economy known for some time before the ousting of Jack Lynch by Charles Haughey in 1979. The 1977 Fianna Fáil election manifesto, on the crest of which McCreevy was himself swept into the Dáil, had all but bankrupted the economy, and McCreevy had been among those who had voted for Haughey, believing him capable of restoring sanity to the national finances. On 11 January 1980, just three days after Charles Haughey's landmark 'We-are-living-beyond-our-means' TV address, McCreevy raged in public about the recent drift of Irish politics. 'General elections seem to be developing into an auction in promises,' he thundered in *Newbridge*. 'We are so hell bent on assuming power that we are prepared to do anything for it.'

In April 1981 McCreevy warned: 'If political parties continue to disgrace themselves, then democracy itself is at risk.' This speech began a process that resulted in his temporary expulsion from the Fianna Fáil parliamentary party, his long-term political estrangement from Haughey and his exclusion from ministerial office for more than a decade. His banishment continued even as the very prescriptions he had been advocating were gradually adopted by the political establishment and media. When Haughey returned to power in February 1987, he had virtually universal support in pursuing the course McCreevy had been banished for promoting. But, although he remained on good personal terms with Haughey, McCreevy languished on the backbenches for another decade, until Albert Reyolds, on replacing Haughey, promoted him to the cabinet.

McCreevy was bright, charismatic and street-smart in a peculiarly Irish, small-town way. A highly skilled communicator, he employed language in a manner deceptively unpolished. Even when he became Minister for Finance, he continued to speak in the imprecise way people speak in shops and restaurants and bars and across garden fences. There was a characteristic about his delivery suggestive of an unaccountable breathlessness. When, as a reporter, you wrote down one of his sentences, you nearly always had to reinterpret it, ever so slightly, maybe by adding in words that he had left out, or because he had forgotten the construction he had embarked upon and ended up with two sentences stuck together like two odd socks at the bottom of the laundry basket. McCreevy's sentences were a wonder of the world. In print, even when edited, they required careful study to decipher. And yet, as he delivered them, they conveyed precisely what he intended.

There is something in the Irish personality that resists pretension and what passes for cosmopolitanism, a resistance to the false. Sometimes this seems to manifest itself as a kind of anti-intellectualism, which causes clever people to conceal their intelligence behind a façade of come-all-ye simplicity. For a politician with intelligence to become and remain electable, it is necessary to sublimate any traits of personality likely to frighten the post-colonial horses. So it is with Charlie McCreevy. His public persona – the bluster, the waffle, the effortless familiarity, the backslapping good humour – were genuine. But they were also carefully – albeit perhaps unconsciously – constructed disguises that enabled him to limbo-dance his way from oblivion to the heights of political power, a kind of Trojan horse for the qualities of good sense and cop-on that McCreevy had in abundance.

McCreevy liked to break down his philosophy into lines that might be thrown across a bar or shouted over the roar of a threshing machine. 'Don't curse the darkness', he would say. 'Turn on the fucking light!'

'I would like to think,' he said near the end of his time as Finance Minster, 'that the approach I've taken, and my economic philosophy, has been . . . that you'll do better with the money in your arse pocket, and make better decisions and put it to better use, than to be feckin' around and goin' in circles and I funnellin' it back out to you some other way. That's a fundamental view of mine. Every other economy that tried any other way of doin' it fell on top of its head. Whereas the economies that've had that particular approach have prospered. So therefore the philosophy of givin' people back their own money has worked in my view, and has contributed to the growth of the Irish economy.'

He railed tautologically against 'left-wing pinkos', but never dreamt of himself as an ideologue. 'But like,' he would say, 'like I've no problem with the socialist system at all, but I've decided over the years, is that people, the whole system works best when people have more freedom in everything. In EVERYTHING. In their own personal lives. Everything.

'There's a core group that . . . and it's anathema to that core group of people that what they have espoused for forty years, since the '60s, of a certain approach, that this other approach, from this bogman from County Kildare, seems to have worked somewhat better. Ninety-eight per cent of them never saw a fuckin' poor day in their lives. They always came from the class that was well privileged, went to the best schools, ate in the best restaurants, and talked to the same people anyway. And people like you and me, and our people, wouldn't be allowed in there. And we all . . . Like. Like. Like. They philosophize and hypothesize and theorize and drink the wine and talk all the night at all the dinner parties, and have these economic philosophies that we'll all be equal and everything else. But they're always more equal than the rest of us. And always could talk down to us about it. And it really kills them that that other type of philosophy has worked.'

In the flood of accusation and rage that followed the meltdown of the Irish economy in 2008, it seemed to go unremarked that the signs of imminent collapse had been there some six years before that. It was also unremarked that, back in 2002, when Charlie

McCreevy announced that the boom was over, he got nothing for his trouble but abuse.

McCreevy had proposed a series of cutbacks in public expenditure he claimed were necessary to rebalance the economy, which he said was beginning to overheat. The press and public went crazy. For once, McCreevy's populist instincts seemed to desert him. On *The Late Late Show*, he was booed by the audience when he tried to justify the measures being taken.

Back in 1982, it had suited the Irish public to have a hero to say sensible things in the nick of time to prevent national bankruptcy. Now, McCreevy, turned gamekeeper, was again demanding the postponement of short-term gratification for long-term benefit. But this time, cushioned by the tiger-fleece of the early Tiger boom, the Irish public wanted the candy to keep on coming. The media, which for many years had led the clamour for the implementation of fiscal rectitude, abandoned economic pieties in favour of a populist witch-hunt. McCreevy threw in the towel and fecked off, like Ray MacSharry before him, to Brussels.

Had he stuck around, would he have repeated his trick of the early 1980s and blown the whistle on a spiralling economy, a spendthrift government, a banking sector out of control? The very idea is almost too tragic to contemplate.

39 Paddy O'Blog

All the time nowadays you meet people, usually males, who tell you there is about to be a revolution. When you do not, in response, begin to nod aggressively in agreement, they then tend to peer at you earnestly. No, they stress, there *really* is going to be a revolution. Don't you know?

What you know, immediately and with certainty, is that yer man is a blogger. He spends every spare minute, and many minutes that he cannot really spare from his personal hygiene routine, thumping aggressively at a keyboard and imagining that he is doing something to change political reality.

Blogging brings out of the cultural undergrowth and into the light the 'bah!' of those whose investment in public action is confined to the hours they spend jerking off in front of computer screens, usually anonymous and always in a disposition of rage and spite. Politically without content and intellectually brain-dead, this cyberspace cornerboyism imagines itself to be hugely sophisticated and threatening to the status quo. Its sense of self-importance is nourished by elements in the mainstream media which have become alert to the possibilities of slipstreaming on the popularity of the web among 'the youth'. In truth, these virtual Don Quixotes do nothing but compete with one another to utter the most immediate and banal opinions in the most poisonous way, but this does nothing to dilute their sense of themselves as plucky and beleaguered dissidents in some repressive dictatorship. In their heart-of-hearts, they long for some totalitarian tyrant to persecute them.

Paddy O'Blog, the Hibernian sub-species of an international phenomenon, is even nastier and more stupid than most of the foreign variations. Pasty-faced and under-sexed, he sits in his darkened room waiting for someone to say or do something, and then he gets to work. He spits fury and indignation like a neurotic Kalashnikov with a jammed trigger mechanism. Everything comes from the top of his head, which is as flat as the earth he inhabits. No inanity is too asinine, no banality too boring for him to hammer vigorously into his keyboard. His first thought on anything becomes his settled opinion, and usually this is received from some other blogger, who just happened to get up a bit earlier and, having nobody to slavishly imitate, delivered himself of the scintillating opinion that George W. Bush is a 'moron' or that Christianity, the civilization which to its sorrow begat him, is 'mumbo jumbo'.

Paddy O'Blog has a limited vocabulary. His compositions are studded with words like 'crap', 'pathetic' and 'arsehole'. He does not think beyond the obvious, but taps out the obvious as though it is the most interesting thing he has ever thought, which very often it is. He is a coward: almost always hiding behind some ridiculous sobriquet, like 'Slugger' or 'Nemesis'. Nobody knows where he lives or anything much about him, other than the opinions he expresses about other people. He is a parasite. He is jealous, mean-spirited, malevolent and petty. He is full of rage and spite. He knows nothing of beauty or love, but only what he hates and whom he envies. No, let us cut to the chase: he knows nothing. He communicates with nobody other than his blogging mates, who are just as ignorant as he is. He considers himself on the same level as journalists who must go out into the world every day, gather information, collect facts, submit themselves to editorial and legal processes, and ultimately take responsibility for every word they write. In fact, a regular theme of his contributions is the idea that he is in the process of supplanting conventional media and making journalists redundant.

This is the only thing he is right about. Because the mainstream media have insisted on seeing the Internet as a cultural as well as a technological 'development' and are afraid of seeming 'out of touch', conventional journalism has been extending an extraordinary level of deference towards O'Blog and his chums. It is a part of the daily cant of journalism that 'citizen journalism', blogging, interactivity and other 'new' forms of communication are changing our democracies, in radical and, it is implied, positive ways. Journalists, terrified of seeming unhip, declare that the bloggers do essentially the same thing as themselves. It does not appear to occur to any of them that the relationship of bloggers to newspapers, for example, is that of a flea to a dog, that the blogger is a parasite who leeches off the 'old' media, especially the printed category, feeding off what the newspapers produce and giving nothing back, but gradually squeezing the life out of that which he subsists on. Newspapers, instead of holding back and allowing the bloggers to choke on their own spite, have opened up their publications, inviting O'Blog to 'comment' on their content – largely unedited and for free!

It is 'interesting', though for dubious reasons, to study the 'threads' which nowadays are attached to many newspaper articles on web editions, like dingleberries from a sheep's arse. These are not neutral conduits for spontaneous opinions, but channels dedicated to forms of mob disgruntlement which has, for perhaps good reasons, no other outlet. Contributors appear to come to the process with a mindset possibly symptomatic of the isolationism involved in Internet communications generally, and anticipating a certain group dynamic. Most contributors appear mostly to want to draw attention to themselves, seeking to convey an impression of strength, cleverness, cynicism or aggressiveness, while pre-empting the possibility of hostility or ridicule by pushing these responses in front like spears. It is often difficult to perceive any intellectual or democratic distinction between most of what they write and the ancient rite of public urination.

Yet, newspapers seem to believe that offering space to P. O'Blog & Co. is a contribution to democracy requiring all conventions and inhibitions to be laid aside. Loyal readers, who carefully consider every aspect of an issue before taking out a writing pad and fountain pen and composing a careful and balanced letter to the editor, are expected to shell out €2 or more for the newspaper, and requested to keep their letters short. But O'Blog can rant and rave at the newspaper's expense for as long as he likes, leeching off its content, insulting its journalists and predicting its imminent demise. If a reader includes in his letter what is euphemistically called a 'four-letter word', it is either excised or disabled by asterisks before publication, yet, on the free website of the same newspaper, O'Blog can refer to 'cock', 'cunts' and 'fuckers' as if he were sitting on a high stool at the bar of his local pub.

As a result, there is now a major crisis in the global newspaper industry. Arising from the complacency and stupidity of the commercial media, bloggers have been enabled to create, for next to nothing, sites in which the content of the professional writer is regurgitated and offered up to the malevolent attentions of O'Blog and his ilk.

Within a short time, this crisis will claim its first casualties in the Irish newspaper industry. It seems not to have occurred to anyone that, if this process runs its projected course, the world will before long be left to the tender mercies of O'Blog and his mates. But, without the 'old' media to leech off, Paddy O'Blog will have nothing to blog about. The 'conventional' media, having been obliterated, will have to be resurrected in an entirely new form, and the old standards and values restored. The public will have to come to realize that, if they want to have decent professional communications, they will have to pay for them. Media organizations will have to find ways to make this work. It would be too much, one supposes, to ask that they and the profession of journalism might find ways of dealing with the problem before it is too late.

40 The Begrudger

For a long time, through good times and bad, perhaps the most maligned species in Irish society was the Begrudger. The case for the prosecution was comprehensively laid out some years ago by Professor J. J. Lee, in his excellent volume, *Ireland 1912–1985: Politics and Society*. Lee credited the Irish with coining the word 'begrudger', but he also argued, in the course of a brilliant mini-essay on the subject, that the documentary evidence of begrudging Irish behaviour was pretty thin on the ground. While noting that it was a tradition of Irish society that 'immense amounts of time were devoted to spiting the other fellow', he also observed that 'the begrudger mentality did derive fairly rationally from a mercantilist concept of the size of the status cake', and that since the size of that cake was more or less fixed, 'one man's gain did tend to be another man's loss'.

It was noticeable that, during the Tiger years, members of the Irish entrepreneurial community employed the concept of begrudgery almost in the manner of a club to beat down even the most tentative hint of criticism concerning the boom and its benefits. Even the merest hint of questioning of their motives, methods or manoeuvrings immediately invited the taunt of 'begrudger', which proved a handy way of discouraging all scrutiny of their activities. To listen to a particular brand of entrepreneur, one would think that the only thing standing between the Irish people and boundless wealth and happiness was this unfortunate tendency to 'begrudge' those who got up at the first burr of the alarm clock and went out to lay two blocks where only one lay before. Those who did not wholeheartedly endorse the entrepreneur's breathtaking path to glory, his *savoir faire*, intelligence and wit, his hale and uninhibited enjoyment of the fruits of his endeavours, were portrayed as malevolent and small-minded, carping sneeringly out of the sides of their mouths about the achievements of their betters. For years, while the Tiger thrived, it was impossible to say a 'bad word' about the handling of the economy without being savaged as a 'begrudger'.

Something interesting happened to journalism also. It's an odd feature of Irish newspapers that, whereas what you might call the engine and chassis of the vehicle is provided by solid economic commentary of an orthodox, market-centred nature, the bodywork is of an entirely different cast. Most of these so-called 'stars' are people who in the old days would have described themselves as socialists and who remain, in spite of improving personal circumstances, of a left-leaning disposition.

Back in the 1980s, it was the height of fashion. All you needed to do was adopt a pessimistic attitude, predict the worst possible outcome for any given aspect of public policy and, above all, accuse the government as often as possible of being wrong-headed and incompetent. Back then, the country was in such a state of chaos that it was impossible to be excessively pessimistic.

But the journalistic doomsters were extremely chagrined by the arrival of the Celtic Tiger. Not only was it neither expected nor predicted, but its arrival, and more especially its timing in the immediate aftermath of the collapse of communism in Eastern Europe, seemed to represent for the doomsters an accusation, suggesting they had been wrong about everything. For years they had been insisting upon the intrinsic unsustainablity and amorality of the capitalist system and predicting the final meltdown of the Irish economy. Now, far from melting, the Irish economy was confounding everything they said and believed, right in front of their eyes. They had no choice but to button it.

Things would have been lean had it not been for the tribunals, but Flood and Moriarty provided an opportunity to transmute the doomsters' ideological pique into a kind of postmodern fiscal puritanism, allowing them to maintain a continuous high moral tone during a period when their portfolios of opinions were otherwise at risk of redundancy.

Thus, the nature of Irish journalism altered fundamentally in the Tiger years, manifesting a dearth of criticism of economic policy, or of issues of societal justice and fairness in a contemporaneous context. Gone were the old journalistic standbys, like attacks on cutbacks in public spending, appeals on behalf of 'the less fortunate in society' and the angry polemic against incompetence in high places. A new tune was created: All Politicians are Crooks and Shysters. Interestingly, this new score related purely to times past, avoiding other than passing and often tortuous reference to the contemporary management of the national affairs, which appeared so unassailable that the erstwhile doomsters had to bite their pencils and keep any doubts to themselves.

Thus, although he was later to re-emerge with the chill winds of recession, the fabled begrudger abandoned Irish society when it needed him most.

As a result of the decades of anti-begrudger propaganda, we tend to identify begrudgery purely with negativity, envy, jealousy and spite. In fact, there may, in the modern world, be a profoundly redemptive quality to this maligned disposition. Back in the 1990s, as the Celtic Tiger was finding its stride, a British clinical psychologist called Oliver James published a book called *Britain on the Couch*, in which he gave rise to the ineluctable inference that what the Irish call begrudgery might be one of the most effective defence mechanisms employed by the delicate human psyche against the seemingly unavoidable tendency of reality to treat different people in an arbitrarily uneven-handed fashion.

Dr James argued that the principal difference between the 1990s and the 1950s was the fact that most or all of us were able to 'know' far, far more people than if we had lived a generation before. Whereas our grandparents 'knew' just their immediate family, neighbours, a small circle of friends and acquaintances, most of us today, courtesy of mass media society, have come to 'know' hundreds, perhaps thousands, of people. This, he argued, has multiplied the effects of our natural tendency to compare ourselves with others. Being surrounded on a daily basis by the manifest 'success' of the rich and famous, we are confronted at all times by the evidence of our own relative failure. This constant, invariably negative comparison, James argued, creates chemical imbalances which attack our self-esteem, confidence and sense of self-possession, creating envy, depression and spiritual malfunction, spawning drug-addictions, obsessive compulsive disorders and insatiable appetites for newer and greater forms of gratification.

Begrudgery, as explained by Professor Lee, is a defence mechanism born of the need to maintain a sense of status and dignity in a society with scarce resources, and may be the only known antidote to this condition. This is why it is a mistake to confuse begrudgery with simple envy or jealousy: a begrudger does not envy the target of his rancid passion; he tears him down, dismisses him and consigns him to oblivion. In the begrudger's denunciation lurks also an annunciation of pride and self-satisfaction which nullifies any danger of succumbing to true envy.

Begrudgery is therefore a cultural form of what Oliver James called 'discounting', which is to say a device to minimize the demoralizing effects of the relative success or attractiveness of others. If upward social comparisons are not to result in a depressing sense of inadequacy, we need to remain mindful of ways in which the object of the negative comparison has been more privileged – or, alternatively, ways in which the envied individual may be disadvantaged – compared to ourselves. The art of the begrudger in remembering the celebrated and successful when they hadn't a pot to piss in becomes, therefore, a device for the preservation of sound mental health and the avoidance of unnecessary feelings of inferiority.

Had the Begrudger been more vocal during the boom time, he may have provided the necessary reality check for those who had power and fortune, and for those among us who furiously, and ultimately unsuccessfully, sought to emulate such status.

41 Bertie Ahern

Bertie may be the last of our leaders whom, instinctively and with ironic good humour, we refer to by his Christian name. Bertie. Albert. Charlie. Garret. All four names have a resonance in Irish politics, echoing backwards over three decades when first names carried significance beyond mere familiarity. This was a period of Irish life which may retrospectively be identified as falling between the reign of the austere father-figure (Dev/Lemass/the Cosgraves) and the coming time of the mere administrator, a period when leaders were lifted up by the force of personal radiance as much as by aptitude or an appetite for power. The coherence of this theory is challenged by a single exception: John Bruton, always 'Bruton', a man who was only partly the victim of a ubiquitous Christian name. He was also a Taoiseach out of sync, never having achieved a popular mandate, and, moreover, seeming to point to that future time when an air of uncharismatic competence would be the defining quality of leadership. Bertie's successor would never be 'Brian', but 'Cowen' or 'Biffo'.

The Bertiness of Bertie, like the Charliness of Charlie, and the Garretness of Garret, is something we're inclined to take for granted. These men did not rise to the top on the basis of ability alone, but more on their capacity to inspire liking, affection, even a kind of love, by insinuating a more intimate relationship with the

voter by tapping into an instinctive connection with a deeper culture.

Most Irish people who were around during the recession of the 1980s regarded the Celtic Tiger as a fraud or an accident. It didn't seem natural or real. Even those who came to embrace it could not quite shake off the suspicion that it had little to do with those guys grinning down from election posters. The thing about Bertie was that he didn't seem to know what was happening either, but somehow came to personify our sense of growing optimism and glee. Although he made interventions from time to time implying that he knew what was going on, nobody ever took these too seriously.

Something changed, then, when we lost faith in Bertie, and it may take a while to perceive exactly what. The disappointment we felt at the end was not merely on account of his failures, which emerged, in retrospect, as legion. It went much deeper than that. Bertie had seemed to have it all sussed. He seemed to do things effortlessly, to possess a sure touch that not merely reassured us as to his competence but made us think that our big mistake all along had been that we were too inclined to see the glass as half empty.

Bertie, with his genius for malapropism, his talent for the unfinished sentence, his mastery of scrambled syntax, radiated something beyond competence, beyond even affability. He created a unique connection with the Irish people by seeming to be remarkably unremarkable in almost every way. He did not draw attention to himself, except by being there, somewhat bemused and diffident, the sheepish Taoiseach. The breadth of his gift for politics was equalled only by its invisibility. Sometimes it seemed that the artifice might be about to reveal itself, but such moments were always ambiguous and fleeting. Bertie was Bertie, and, even though this condition baffled every attempt at description, we fancied we had come to comprehend how it moved and what it meant.

Bertie Ahern and Tony Blair, the two leaders on these neigh-bouring islands in the boom times coinciding with the advent of the third millennium, were stars in bright skies, both belonging more to show business than politics. The external conditions somehow conspired to ensure that both could shine, that nothing could break the illusion of the performance. Blair and Ahern made it look easy in a way that Brown and Cowen, even given similar conditions, would have been unable to match. Things might have gone just as swimmingly, but we would not have felt quite so self-satisfied about it.

Bertie and the way he might look at you. Bertie, who made it all seem so easy. Bertie, who might tell the odd porky, but wouldn't do you a bad turn.

Stay cool, he seemed to say, in the very timbre of his voice. So, we stayed cool and started to believe in the miracle. What did Bertie stand for? Erm? What were his guiding ideas? Dunno. Bertie took the helm at a time when all the pieces were clicking together. He held the tiller steady enough to see out his own time before the whole thing went mushroom-shaped.

For just over a decade, Bertie Ahern grinned down at us as if to say: 'Jaze, who'dave ever've taut it'd get so good?' And then the bills came in.

There is a fantastic gothic novel by Patrick McGrath called *Dr Haggard's Disease*, in which the eponymous protagonist, lovesick and isolated, goes slowly insane. Early in the story he seems perfectly stable, but by the end is clearly barking. And yet there is no clear tipping point, no definitive event, epitomizing or signalling a clear beginning to this process. By the time it begins to dawn on the reader that this character has actually been mad from the beginning, there is a sense not only of being taken in but of actually being conjoined in the doctor's madness.

The Bertie Ahern saga is like that. At the outset of his joust with the Mahon Tribunal, when his explanations for his sudden windfalls of unaccounted and unbanked cash tended to hinge on the breakdown of his marriage, it was perhaps understandable that people would support him. Things began to get a little flaky after that, but still, in a certain light, his accounts of his bookkeeping and banking practices fell within the bounds of comprehensibility for those of us who can't remember what we did with our wages last month, never mind a decade ago. Comprehensible, that is, provided you soft-focused the fact that, at all relevant times, Bertie was the Minister for Finance.

And if you took into account, as he never tired of hinting, that the tribunal process was driven by his political enemies, the idea of Bertie as persecuted innocent had a degree of plausibility. But inexorably the inconsistencies piled up and his multiple-choice explanations created a gridlock of scepticism that gradually vindicated those who had proposed a simple explanation from the beginning: Bertie was as dodgy as a nine-euro note.

Bertie's mentor and notorious predecessor, Charles Haughey, was, in a certain sense, corrupt, but he was also unlucky. Bertie was lucky enough to lead in tumultuous times, which meant that he created a vast credit of indulgence for when the tribunal came knocking. Interestingly, the growing public incredulity concerning his evidence seemed to parallel pretty precisely the ominous rumblings of the coming recession.

While everything was going well, a little bit of how's-your-father may have seemed like grease for the wheels of development and prosperity. But, with the boom over and a growing sense that we have little enough to show for it, there began to develop a palpable public feeling that, as the story of Bertie's financial misadventures essayed a slow slide into farce, we were watching a dramatization of something much larger and much more ominous.

At each stage of the story, until the very end, it had been possible to leave open the merest chink of doubt. Taken in isolation, every one of his explanations had a certain ring of plausibility, though for those who zeroed in on the detail, the big picture became increasingly and embarrassingly irrefutable. Finally, as Bertie straightfacedly told the tribunal about his incredible run of betting coups and windfalls, the penny began to drop for even the most myopically loyal. The cats' laughter from the gallery in Dublin Castle, as Bertie sought to weave yet another version of his financial good fortune, provided a most articulate summary of public attitudes. Before long, the implosion of the economy seemed to replicate the mess of Bertie's personal finances, and we came to the ineluctable conclusions.

In the end we regarded him much as the wife and children of a polygamist might do on hearing that Daddy had four other families in various parts of the city. Our affection for Bertie had been total at times. And so the emergence of the truth about his miraculous powers meant, really, that we could never love again.

Declan Ganley

I t was late 2007 when Libertas first began to be mentioned. It all seemed very odd. People had been used to all kinds of stray elements, usually from the far left or right, becoming involved in EU debates, but the idea of a wealthy businessman doing so was odd in the extreme. Why would someone like Declan Ganley want to pull down a European treaty? What sort of businessman could afford to take time off from his business to do for nothing the kind of stuff politicians were paid to do? There were all kinds of rumours about Ganley's connections to all kinds of interests and operators, but nothing ever emerged to definitively answer the question.

Back in 1972, 211,891 Irish people (17 per cent of the population) had voted against joining the 'Common Market'. Many of these people believed membership would lead to the destruction of the Irish farming and fishing industries, and make us the paupers of Europe. They insisted that the required trade-offs – especially the exchange of sovereignty and natural resources for infrastructure – would erode our long-term capacity for self-sufficiency. Over the years, these arguments continued to be canvassed, but were treated with increasing scepticism and impatience as Ireland began to experience the benefits of European partnership.

Whether we agreed with it or not, the decision to join the Common Market seemed to have set us on a path that could not be retraced. With ratification of the Maastricht Treaty, in 1992, we seemed to cross over into a new idea of Ireland, accepting a different relationship with the rest of Europe. With that treaty, the EU ceased to be merely a co-operative community, acquiring many of the characteristics of a single political entity. It might have been assumed that, in voting Yes to Maastricht, the Irish electorate was aware of the choice it was making. It seemed obvious that the argument for an independent Ireland had been lost. It also seemed obvious that our pursuit of a particular approach to economic development had left us no longer in a position to be choosers. Ireland had become so dependent on the relationship with the community that, henceforth, almost everything that concerned our future would have to be pursued from an acceptance of this dependence.

In 2008, when the Lisbon Treaty came up for ratification, the indigenous economy was largely secondary to a kind of cuckoo-in-the-nest multinational economy operating on the spoils of Ireland as a trade-off for employment. The national economic strategy, such as it was, depended mainly on outsiders coming in and creating activity from which we gained temporary benefits. The economic model we had chosen depended on us being part of the European Union. Nobody among our political class offered any vision by which we might proceed outside the EU or in a reduced role within it. We might smugly declare that we were 'all Europeans now', but we had no interest in anything but the dosh.

But an element of cussedness had crept into the electoral mindset during the Tiger years. Perhaps arising from cockiness or relative dissatisfaction with how the spoils of prosperity were dividing up, the sentiment of the average citizen appeared to lurch occasionally towards a kind of neurosis. This may have been one of the legacies of a decade of revelations about the financial improprieties of members of the political class. Suspicion and paranoia ruled, but there was also something even more fundamental, bordering on a visceral dislike of the political animal, and anyone who could stoke the fires of suspicion – as Declan Ganley and Libertas managed to do – had a good chance of giving the political establishment a run for its money.

This new sentiment was not confined to radicals or young people or any of the other standard disgruntled constituencies. It was to be found in all elements of Irish society – for example, in people who a generation before were part of what appeared to be an overwhelming moral majority in favour of Ireland's participation in the European project. The 2008 referendum, for example, was dominated by the emergence of a band of media commentators opposed to Lisbon who, in every previous referendum, had been unquestioning cheerleaders for the political class.

Opposition to Lisbon was not, we were assured, directed at the European Union *per se*, but only to particular aspects, although nobody seemed sure which ones. There were vague fears about increasing bureaucratic encroachment and the loss of autonomy in legal and fiscal affairs, but the most effective slogan of the campaign was 'If you don't know, vote no'. Many of those who voted against the treaty subsequently admitted they did so because they did not understand it. Others referred to alleged provisions in the text with implications for Irish neutrality, taxation or abortion, which had no more validity than in any of the previous referendums concerning aspects of EU membership. The plain truth – that the Lisbon Treaty was simply a series of complicated but anodyne technical measures, a nut-tightening exercise following recent expansions – was not believed by large numbers of people.

After it was all over, there was no sense of exhilaration or achievement, other than among a tiny proportion of activists of the

extreme left and right. It is as though we found ourselves in the
moment of realization after a heated but meaningless row, when
the parties look into each other's eyes with a feeling of
embarrassment and dawning awareness. There was a sense that the
frenzy of the moment had taken things too far, and now we had to
sweep up the broken crockery. A survey conducted by the
European Commission immediately after the vote revealed that
many people who did not understand the treaty voted No; that the
overwhelming majority of women voted No; that young people
voted No by a margin of two to one; and that immigration (i.e.
xenophobic sentiment) was a significant factor. It was difficult to
escape the conclusion that the Irish had voted No because of
irrelevancies, or marginal issues, or, in many instances, just plain
spite, pique or ignorance. There was even a feeling that many
people voted No in the belief that enough people would vote Yes to
absolve them of responsibility for the consequences of their empty,
petulant gestures.

The outcome seemed to articulate something much darker than
anything remotely to do with the treaty, a kind of fury with no
precise centre. It is as though Lisbon acted as a poultice to draw out
a whole range of festering resentments, many unspecified and even
publicly denied.

Declan Ganley was the main agent in this occurrence. And yet,
twelve months later, in the summer of 2009, the non-ignition of
Libertas was one of the most striking outcomes of the European
elections. With the Lisbon issue still unresolved, and indeed with the
victory chants that followed the 2008 Lisbon result still ringing in his
ears, Ganley was himself defeated in the North-West constituency,
and none of his fellow Libertas candidates got a look-in.

Ganley, of course, was not the kind of figure who tends to attract
approval in the heartlands of Connacht; a self-made businessman

with a plummy accent who had not served his time in service to the tribe. Though adept at tailoring his message to tap into the various disgruntlements that were current in a time of growing economic upheaval, he lacked any real empathy with the people he was addressing. Though possessed of a formidable array of insights into the history of Ireland's relationship with Europe, he never succeeded in obtaining real traction for his ambitions, whatever they were.

In the end, Declan Ganley probably did more to set back any possibility of a real engagement with the deeper issues of the European project than if he had never intervened at all. For some time to come, anyone seeking to raise these issues will be immediately struck down in the public imagination as coming 'after Ganley' – who came, saw, was defeated and gave up. As a result, Irish Euro-scepticism faces the prospect of going down in history as a briefly flowering hubris arising from prosperity, just one more example of how we lost the run of ourselves.

43 Judge Mary Fahy

Once upon a time, Good Friday was a day of peace and quiet. For religious reasons, it was an exceptional day, but that was not the whole of the story. It was a day, perhaps the only day, when people were able to reclaim a sense of innocence. Because the pubs were closed and you weren't supposed to eat meat, everybody knuckled down to doing a bit of penance and grumbling only a little. Secretly, most people felt okay about it. The pubs were shut, so it was the only day of the year when you had a good excuse for not drinking. Christmas Day, the other day the pubs were shut, didn't count, for obvious reasons. Whenever someone complained about not being able to get hammered on Good Friday, only idiots made a fuss about it. Most people just shrugged, shook their heads and thanked their lucky stars there was one day that was genuinely special. Maybe they could sneak into church without anyone seeing them and re-enter their childhoods, when the shops had closed and only the emergency services were working. There was a double benefit: a sense of being at peace with the world and the feeling that you could really enjoy having a good drink on Easter Sunday, when purity-of-conscience would make it taste ten times better.

All this is gone. Good Friday is now pretty much the same as any other day, and in a couple more years there will be no difference at all. In 2010, a district court judge decided that, because there was a big rugby match in Limerick on Good Friday, the pubs should be allowed to open after six p.m. Judge Tom O'Donnell ruled in favour of an application by the city's Vintners Federation who said they stood to lose a fortune if they couldn't open that day. 'I accept that this decision may cause controversy in several quarters,' he said, 'and, having considered the arguments, I wish to point out that the district court is a court of record and not a court of precedent.' Noting that Thomond Park, where the game was to take place, held a special arena licence which allowed alcohol to be served, the judge said that it was 'somewhat absurd' that the pubs in the locality should be closed while 26,000 people were free to buy alcohol in the grounds.

Certainly, this was one potential absurdity. Another was the idea that 26,000 people appeared to contemplate with fear the idea of having to attend a rugby match without getting hammered out of their skulls. Still another was that here, yet again, was a judge of the lowest court in the land making a decision that, legal precedent or not, was likely to lead to a further erosion of a tradition that nobody had ever voted to dismantle.

This is how laws get made or changed in modern Ireland. Politicians slide about the place, trying not to make decisions that might offend or irritate anybody, and judges step into the breach and decide things on the hoof. In fairness to Judge O'Donnell, he was confronted with an application for a 'special event' licence, and the match, which apparently could not be played on any other day, constituted such an event. The judge said he had heard 'compelling evidence' concerning the importance of the event to the hotel industry. He observed that there was no statutory definition of what constituted a 'special event'. He appeared to be genuinely seeking a solution that would meet the exceptional circumstances without delivering a fatal blow to an ancient and sacred tradition against which he himself appeared to have no gripe.

This is more than can be said for Judge Mary Fahy, who, presiding at Galway District Court in 2008, refused to record convictions in nine cases in which restaurants were prosecuted for serving wine on Good Friday that year. Prosecuting restaurants for offering wine to their customers with their meals on Good Friday was 'ludicrous' and 'ridiculous', she said. People were 'entitled' to have wine with their meals. Judge Fahy marked the facts proven in all cases but recorded no convictions. She said that, while the state and the garda were 'technically correct' in bringing the prosecutions under the intoxicating liquor legislation, she would not be happy to record convictions. She observed that she was probably leaving herself open to judicial review by the state for taking this stance, but she didn't mind.

'If people want to go out for a meal on Good Friday, I would have thought they could have a drink with their meal,' she said. 'Technically you [the garda inspector who had brought the prosecution] are correct, but I think myself it is absolutely ludicrous that people on holidays especially cannot have a glass of wine with their meal. I'm not advocating that pubs open on Good Friday but I think restaurants should open.'

It is difficult to know where to start with this farrago of presumption and arrogance. The fact is that, regardless of what Judge Mary Fahy or anyone else thinks of it, the Intoxicating Liquor Act makes clear that people are not entitled to have wine with their meals on Good Friday, unless they choose to eat in private, in which case they may do as they please. The law makes it explicitly clear that Good Friday is one of two days in the year on which it is forbidden to sell alcohol in public. The background to why this is so, and whether it is a good idea, may well make for interesting material for debate, but such discussion has no place in a court of law. Whether it is a good or a bad idea for people to have a glass of wine with their meals on Good Friday is none of Judge Mary Fahy's concern when she is sitting as a judge in Galway District Court. She is there in that capacity to implement the law, without fear or favour, having taken a solemn oath to do precisely that. Her sole function in court is to know the law and follow it to the letter. Whether she believes a law to be ludicrous, ridiculous or otherwise is of no relevance. She is neither a TD sitting in Dáil Éireann, nor a Senator sitting in Seanad Éireann. Nor is she the President of the Republic, with discretion as to which laws she will sign into law and which she will refer to the Supreme Court.

When Judge Fahy told the prosecuting garda inspector that he was 'technically' correct, she was engaging in a form of semantics. The law recognizes no other kind of correctness but technical correctness. The garda inspector was there doing his job, implementing the law as he, just like Judge Fahy, was obliged by his calling to do. He was correct, full stop.

Of course, nobody was surprised that, in making these statements from the bench, she was applauded by certain elements in an increasingly alcohol-obsessed society as a voice of reason. In this wet-brained Ireland, anyone who supports the alleged freedom of the citizen to obtain full access to his or her drug-of-choice is likely to be feted as a hero or heroine. Thus, it was not surprising that the central meaning of what occurred at Galway District Court would be obscured or ignored. In this she was utterly vindicated by the subsequent public commentary. The 'liberal', anti-Catholic gallery, delighted that someone had sought to remove from it the terrible yoke of enforced public sobriety on Good Fridays, seemed not to care that what had happened in this episode was that a judge had refused to do what she was employed to do, and that the implications of this were, you might say, staggering.

44 Owen Keegan

Once upon a time, it was possible to walk around an urban thoroughfare in Ireland and not fear your day being destroyed by remorseless men in uniform. Nowadays, however, to meet a fellow citizen in the street is to encounter a shadow of a man or woman, unable to conduct a civil conversation without constantly consulting a timepiece.

Few events in recent history have illustrated the supine, defeated state of the Irish public as comprehensively as the introduction to Irish cities of wheel clamping. The general response to this outrage was at the time characterized by casual submissiveness and an almost sadomasochistic fascination with the clamping device itself. Those who operate this monstrous insult to public liberty informed us, courtesy of the media, that the public's response was proving to be 'generally very good'. Most people had been understanding, we were told, of the necessity to 'free up' the capital's traffic system. Those who fell victim to this appalling abuse of their rights were philosophical, accepting their medicine with polite resignation. The law was the law, after all.

Let us be absolutely clear. The introduction of wheel clamping in Dublin had nothing at all – repeat, nothing at all – to do with easing traffic congestion. It had to do, and only to do, with extracting even more money from motorists, who were already paying through the nose, ears, eyes and other orifices for the privilege of owning cars. A leaflet distributed to Dublin households by Dublin Corporation, as part of its highly successful public relations campaign to justify the importation of this outrageous practice, described wheel clamping as a 'traffic-management measure' and claimed that 'illegal parking restricts traffic movement and causes congestion'. Even if this were always true, which it is not, it would not amount to a justification of the introduction of wheel clamping. Illegally parked cars which restrict traffic movement and cause congestion were not the kind of illegally parked cars being clamped under this new, inhuman regime, which zeroed in on easy targets: people who overstayed their time by a few minutes in a parking bay, or who overslept in the morning and come downstairs to encounter a yellow encumbrance adhering to their mode of transport. Wheel clamping was not a 'traffic-management measure', but a form of extortion.

The previous system of parking tickets was at least redeemed by some elements of humanity. Traffic wardens were usually vaguely human, and could be appealed to on that basis. Moreover, they had systems, which could be cracked. Once you figured out how a particular warden operated, it was possible to lengthen the odds on obtaining a penalty by various stratagems which are now, sadly, about to become obsolete. Under the old system, you sometimes won and sometimes lost, but generally speaking the system was fair, reasonable and flexible. The clamping regime left no prospect of escape, being inhuman not merely in its consequences, but also in its demeanour, in its imperviousness to human intervention. What had always been a blood sport became the equivalent of hare coursing.

Wheel clamping, of course, like so much else of our public policy, was an idea imported from Britain – imitation being the most noticeable talent of those who run our public affairs. It would never, of course, occur to such people to look at the broader context in which wheel clamping is implemented in Britain – the fact, for example, that it is combined with the benefits of a functioning public transport system. Wheel clamping has been in force in London for many years, but there is virtually no place in London where one is more than ten minutes' walk from an Underground station, a system rendering any area of a vast metropolis reachable within an hour.

If an Englishman's home is his castle, an Irishman's car is his chariot, his indispensable ally in moving about his benighted island home. In Dublin there is, for most people, no alternative to driving into the city. Visitors to our capital city choke in disbelief when informed that there is no rail link between Dublin city centre and Dublin airport, a neglect which has led to half of north Dublin being turned into a car park and made the process of parking a car at the airport more time-consuming than the air journey between Dublin and London. The very same authorities which recently introduced wheel clamping have for decades stonewalled attempts to progress with any form of underground or light rail system for Dublin. The same people who have wined and dined and winked and nodded with lobbyists for the road and motor industries, now lecture us about our dependency on the motor car.

The man to ultimately blame is Owen Keegan. From the very moment of his appointment as head of traffic with Dublin Corporation, it began to seem obvious that Mr Keegan did not like motor vehicles very much. He introduced a series of traffic restrictions in Dublin with no apparent purpose but to drive drivers mad. Once, for example, you could turn right from South Great George's Street on to Dame Street. At a stroke of Mr Keegan's pen, this simple manoeuvre was arbitrarily outlawed, and anyone wanting to access College Green from South Great George's Street had to detour around Christ Church and up along the quays. In any other context, apparent doltishness would be seen for what it is, but Mr Keegan was knowingly playing to a gallery of bicycle-clipped commentators guaranteed to hail every attempt to stick it to the motorist, regardless of legality or sense.

For years, Irish car owners had been browbeaten into believing that they are a class of neo-criminals who poison the atmosphere, endanger public safety and block the roads. That they have been made to believe this, while simultaneously being forced to pay for these selfsame roads, was an awesome feat of public indoctrination. That car drivers had been persuaded that traffic chaos in Dublin and elsewhere was the result of their selfishness, their lack of public spirit, was one of the great wonders of the modern world.

In a modern society, a motor car is, for better or worse, an extension of the self, an essential means of getting about and taking care of business and responsibility. To clamp the motor vehicle of a citizen, therefore, is tantamount to withdrawing that person's liberty for the purpose of revenue collection. It is unthinkable that even unelected bureaucrats like Owen Keegan could succeed in the reintroduction of the stocks. Yet citizens stand disconsolately by as this menace to society stealthily introduces a tyranny just as immobilizing of personal liberty, and therefore equally monstrous.

45 Ryan Tubridy

Somewhere, deep in the pancreas of RTE is a memo which goes something like this: 'If Gay Byrne's contribution was to the modernization of Irish society, that of his successor must be to its postmodernization.' Since there is dispute among cultural commentators about the precise meaning of the term, we should perhaps declare that an Irish postmodernist is someone who doesn't give a shite about anything. In television terms, it is someone with a talent for running up and down steps carrying a phallus-shaped microphone, asking 'wacky' questions of the audience.

RTE, like most organizations in today's Ireland, is run by fogeys of various ages, mostly the older variety, who desire, above all, to hold on to their positions of influence. But there is a problem: all these Young People are drifting about out there and feck knows what they'd be thinking about. All we know is they like comedy, drink, Internet chatrooms, headbanging music and drugs that make them jump about uncontrollably. Obviously, whoever would inherit the mantle of the Great Gaybo should be someone with some clue about what makes them feckers 'tick'. The fogeys' objective was to give the younger generations influence without power, so that fogeyism could remain in control until well into the third millennium.

Pat Kenny was half-right when, before he took it on and spent a decade driving it into the ground, he said that, following Gaybo's departure, *The Late Late* should be 'parked'. In fact, it should have been clamped, towed away, stripped to its chassis and melted down for scrap.

The ethos of *The Late Late*, up until the end of the second millennium, implied some level of concern about Irish society. For *The Late Late* to prosper, it was necessary for the audience to believe that Ireland was something more than a piece of ground on which various activities – work, drinking, dancing, sex – might take place. But nobody will ever again care as much about Ireland as the post-emergency generations who wasted their youths talking about it, and no future presenter of *The Late Late* could possibly tolerate the level of hype which Uncle Gaybo, acting as Father Confessor to this obsessive generation, brought to bear on the subject.

There was a time, coinciding with the heyday of *The Late Late*, when it was possible to talk without irony about television having an 'impact' on something called 'Irish society'. Now it is not possible to talk without irony about anything. To retain credibility as a Young Person today, it is essential that you know as little as possible about issues of public importance. Knowing the name of the incumbent Taoiseach, never mind the names of his predecessors, is a complete no-no. Young people today don't give a blogger's fart about 'Irish society', still less know why they should spend their Friday nights watching it being impacted upon. Neither do they believe television has any business conducting 'debates'. Television is there to make you laugh, to sell you things, to dull the ache in your left temple, to keep boredom at bay and to sober you up for the next party. This condition, which once we would have called apathy, has been formed largely by the fogeys' determination to devolve use of the media without devolving power. To maintain fogery in power, the coming generation of fogeys is to be given fame without influence, to be allowed on television but not to put it to any use. And this suits the young fogeys fine.

Ryan Tubridy is the answer to the old fogeys' wet dreams: a young fogey who is interested in the rewards of television without caring much about its power. He is a kind of postmodern Gaybo in that he has the patter down pat and much better than Pat.

Even before he got the job, Ryan Tubridy talked about not wanting to have 'long-winded curent affairs debates' on his *Late Late*. Then, in the next breath, he insisted that he was a serious guy. Tubridy is extremely bright, in the sense that he has a sharp intelligence and a natural curiosity. He is extraordinarily, genuinely, likeable, and this allows him to get away with things almost nobody else could. His personality conceals how hard he has worked to make himself look like a natural. He also knows something about stuff – politics, books, movies, celebrity fluff – but perhaps not enough about anything to be really lethal. On the debit side, he seems far too concerned about what people think of him, especially people of his own generation, most of whom he seems to think brighter than himself. This creates a wariness of depth that causes his hoe more often to merely scratch the surface of things, where Gaybo's cut deep and sure. This tendency has emerged in his very first programme, in an interview with the Taoiseach, Brian Cowen, when Tubridy seemed more interested in asking hard questions than getting interesting answers.

In his very first show as *Late Late* presenter, in September 2009, he interviewed Brian Cowen, on the defensive after a rough fifteen months as Taoiseach. It was, on the surface, an uncompromising interview. Tubridy asked several are-you-still-beating-your-wife questions. Was he sorry for anything? Would he apologize for his mistakes? Was that an apology or not? Cowen was asked about

NAMA and Bertie's perfect timing and whether he, Cowen, actually enjoyed being Taoiseach. Did he ever wake up and ask, 'Why me?'

But often it seemed that Tubridy was asking questions for the sake of asking them, rather than for the answers – as though he wanted above all to avoid the accusation that he had dodged putting his man on the spot. A potentially car-crash question about the Taoiseach's drinking came wrapped up in a standard 'what-do-you-say-to-those-who . . .?' formulation, with Tubridy fingering a Sunday newspaper for already raising the issue, and then all but apologizing for asking. Was he, he wondered aloud, annoying Cowen? Maybe, he mused just as Cowen started to answer, it was too personal a question? It was impossible to avoid the suspicion that Tubridy seemed to want to retain Cowen's affections more than he needed to get real answers. And yet, the ostensible impression was of a tough interview in which Cowen was asked things he hadn't been asked before.

The core problem with Tubridy is that he seems to be aware mainly of the prestige and celebrity status of his position as *Late Late* host, as opposed to having a sense of the meaning and importance of the show as a cultural lever. He wants to be an Irish Letterman, but without any sense of what, other than imitation, this might involve. Tubridy always wanted to be a broadcaster, but it is as yet by no means clear what he wanted to be a broadcaster for. There is no sense of a mission, other than to be 'on the radio' or 'on the telly', saying stuff. He is extremely good at it, at effecting an impersonation of a great broadcaster operating at the centre of his society, but he has yet to discover what he wants to do with that power.

In this he is quintessentially representative of his generation, which is fascinated with the cultural mechanisms it inherited but unable to put them to any use. Tubridy will never become the greatest Irish broadcaster of the twenty-first century by coasting in the slipstream created by the giants who preceded him, never taking anything seriously enough to seem 'uncool'. He may go on being able to fake it for a while. But unless, while that red light glows, he engages with the stuff of the society – the very things that, glancing towards his gallery, he dismisses as 'long-winded' – he will never be anything but a magpie who picks up fascinating thoughts, looks at them in wry wonder and throws them away. And in a while it will show. Nobody will be able to say what the problem is, but one day people will begin to mutter that Ryan Tubridy, who once seemed so promising, has become sooo yesterday.

46 Seanie FitzPatrick

Reviewing the damage done in hard currency, and perceiving the disaster in terms of its final playing out, it would be possible, without attracting much in the way of criticism or dissent, to fill any list of fifty feckers who fecked up Ireland with the names of fifty bankers.

In the case of Seanie FitzPatrick, former Chairman of Anglo Irish Bank, the amounts of folding stuff involved are so gargantuan as to make it a plausible proposition that Seanie was single-handedly responsible for the collapse of the Irish economy and the pauperizing of at least two generations of Irish people.

To make it worse, if such were possible, it emerged that Seanie had for years been doctoring the accounts at Anglo Irish Bank to make it appear that the bank was more solvent than it was. Sleights of hand were used to 'flatter' the balance sheets, with major customers being encouraged to make short-term lodgements coming up to the end of the financial year. These 'bed and breakfast' arrangements gave the impression of a healthy rate of deposits, which kept the regulators and credit agencies happy.

It gradually emerged that this practice of 'balance sheet management' was widespread in the Irish banking sector. Seanie, of course, not being a man to do things by halves, had taken the device to the level of high art. He had himself borrowed some €85 million

from his own bank, of which €68 million had been written off by the obliging management. Other directors had borrowed a total of €56 million, of which some €40 million had been written off.

It's known as the 'Celtic Chernobyl'. The figures, no matter how you cut them, were beyond belief. The banking crisis would cost every family in Ireland something like €2,000 a year for far longer than anyone could foresee, the equivalent of €50,000 added to every mortgage in the land. All Irish banks were disaster areas, but Anglo Irish was the worst, accounting for debts of €40 billion and rising by the day. It was as if nothing that had happened in Ireland for the previous fifteen years – or indeed for the seventy-five years or so before that – had had any purpose or merit at all. Everything had come not just to nothing, but to a lot less than nothing.

And the madness had been facilitated and enabled by those whose job it was to ensure that the banking sector was adequately regulated and monitored. In September 2008, less than a fortnight before the government announced that it would guarantee all debts and deposits in Irish banks, the then Financial Regulator, Mr Patrick Neary, had declared that Irish banks were 'resilient and well capitalized'.

Nobody could understand why we couldn't just close down Anglo. It was not as though we could not manage without a bank that was costing us several years' worth of GDP to keep the doors open. But the Taoiseach and his Minister for Finance patiently explained that it was because of the bond-holders and our international creditworthiness. Nobody would lend us any more money unless we paid off what we had already borrowed. Still, nobody could understand. What? – we needed to go broke in order to stop ourselves going broke?

Sean FitzPatrick was now a national pariah. Every day, the newspapers carried stories about his €100,000-a-year membership of a golf club in Marbella and his cars and his pension plans and the fact that, as a former director of Aer Lingus, he still got free flights. The people of Ireland became madder and madder until it seemed they would burst. A newspaper carried a front-page picture one day of Seanie and another famous Irish banker, Michael 'Fingers' Fingleton, boss of Irish Nationwide, with the headline, 'They Should be Shot'. A radio show invited people to text in their responses and almost everyone agreed. The editor went on television and said that, of course, it wasn't meant literally, that it was, of course, a popular colloquialism used to express strong emotions.

Seanie made a plausible scapegoat. His raffish good looks and expensive mode of dress made him easy to hate. When he was brought in for questioning to Bray Garda station, he emerged, after the maximum statutory period allowed for questioning, wearing a smart blazer, shirt and tie. Even in ignominy, he seemed to have lost none of the arrogance that had made him the most beloved of bankers in the Tiger years. No longer plain 'Sean', he became 'Seanie', the mock-palsy inflection of that 'e'-sound managing to summon up an immeasurable amount of cultural rage and contempt.

But Seanie had been, in many respects, the epitome of the Celtic Tiger breed. He had pursued, perhaps slightly harder than others, the ethic that had driven the Irish economy from success to triumphalism, simply translating the mindset of the Tiger years into a fit-for-purpose banking model. In 2007, the year before it collapsed, Anglo Irish Bank, with shares peaking at €17.31, was held up as a model for other banks to follow. FitzPatrick was amenable to business people in search of start-up capital – oblivious, it seemed, that this would one day read as 'reckless lending'. Minimal regulation sang a two-part harmony with a degree of faith in the future that, had the whole thing not been a house of cards, would have made Seanie a candidate for canonization.

It became fashionable, after the collapse of the Celtic Tiger, for people to begin their remarks about the catastrophe by emphasizing that they did not go in for 'this "we" business'. By this they meant that they did not accept, for themselves or those for whom they purported to speak, any portion of the blame for the madness that had gripped the country for most of the aptly named Noughties. Of course, most Irish people did not get rich in those years, and many had as much of a struggle as they'd ever had. But there was, none the less, a collective element to the madness that, in retrospect, few seemed willing to own up to. In those years, the Irish people, generally speaking, began to feel that the hand of history, which had hitherto offered them the hind tit in everything, had suddenly changed its attitude. After 800 years of poverty and abuse, they were being offered an opportunity to have a decent life and a comfortable old age. Not alone did nothing or nobody suggest that this perception was fundamentally wrong, but any residual doubts or caution were scoffed away by 'experts' speaking daily on the media platforms from which the same experts would later pronounce on the crimes of the bankers, developers and politicians. Money was now 'cheap', they assured us, cheaper than it had ever been before. In fact, it was so cheap that someone who had borrowed lots of it was far better off than someone who had borrowed nothing. The same newspapers that would later condemn Seanie, Fingers *et al.* were daily running graphs showing how much property had gone up since last month/last week/yesterday. The most modest householder was encouraged to think of himself as a shrewd speculator, whose house was 'earning' multiples of whatever he himself was bringing home. It therefore followed – did it not? – that said householder could treat his income as pin money, to be thrown around without a second thought? In fact, why not take out a credit card so as not to be hidebound by anything as tedious as earned income?

This is what happened, whether we like to admit it or not. Not everyone was equally 'guilty'. Perhaps nobody, in truth, was as 'guilty' as Seanie Fitz. But Seanie's sins were not purely his own. They were the sins of a culture out of control.

In a culture gone clean out of its mind, there was always going to be someone slightly, or even considerably, more barefaced than everyone else. The Anglo figures were spectacular, but, had this particular atrocity not happened, everyone would have been just as outraged by what, thanks to Seanie, seemed the more modest craziness of AIB or Bank of Ireland.

There was always going to be a villain, and Seanie, to give him his due, made for a good one – well turned out and unrepentant to the end.

47 George Lee

In early May 2009, when George Lee announced that he was leaving RTE to run for Fine Gael, the idea began to take root in the Irish consciousness that George could become the answer to all our problems. This being just four months after the inauguration of Barack Obama as President of the United States, the notion of finding a fresh young hero was something to get carried away by. The fact that George wasn't black was just the beginning of the problem.

George was already a national icon from his frequent reports on the state of the economy on radio and television. These were always clear and factual, and frequently offered devastating indictments of the government's stewardship of the national fortunes. George was the bespectacled boy who had a dream about the emperor's Finance Minister with no backside in his trousers, and shouted it out on the six o'clock news. This made George a good economics reporter, but not necessarily a good national saviour.

Having George join its ranks might have been enough to suggest that Fine Gael was the answer to all our problems, which, for all the awfulness of the incumbent government, would have been stretching things. But by then, the Irish people were so desperate for answers they would have pulled the arm off anyone who seemed to know anything and was prepared to talk intelligently about it.

Apart from his undoubted capability as an economic analyst,

there was something endearing about George. He had fire in his belly. He appeared to be sincere in his belief that the Cowen administration was the worst in the history of the State. His declaration that he wanted to be able to tell his children that when his country was in trouble he 'got involved and tried to fix things' resonated with many of his fellow citizens, despite the growing cynicism of the times.

In newspaper articles shortly after he announced that he would be a candidate for Fine Gael in an upcoming by-election in Dublin South, George outlined his manifesto for saving Ireland. He attacked the government for its record, just as he had when he was Economics Editor of RTE, but did not seem to realize that, as a politician, he would need to go further than criticism. George said that unemployment had doubled in the previous year and predicted that it might approach 600,000 by the end of 2009. But he offered no plan to create jobs. He said the government had offered no hope, but he did not have any hopeful thoughts of his own. With an election to fight and a half-page in a national newspaper to play with, you might have expected George to come right out and say what he proposed to do differently. But he didn't. He just said we needed an energetic new government, 'capable of fresh thinking' and 'strong enough to drive change'. But what kind of fresh thinking seemed unclear and he didn't seem to be thinking many fresh thoughts.

George criticized a recent emergency Budget, with its savage tax hikes, cuts in welfare and mortgage relief and its promise of a property tax. 'This is not acceptable,' George emphatically declared. But he did not say what he *would* accept. People might have been forgiven for thinking that, if George had a realistic alternative to all this misery, he should not go on keeping it to himself, but should spit it out so we could all get back to the party.

Then, briefly, it seemed that George might be about to suggest something concrete. While the rest of the world was engaged in expanding public investment and cutting taxes, the government was doing the opposite and was therefore making things worse, he explained. This was taking billions of euros out of the economy at the wrong time, and would ensure the downturn lasted much longer than anything we had seen until then. It would stifle hope, discourage enterprise and could 'easily turn a recession into a depression'.

You didn't need to have been the Economics Editor of RTE to know this. For nearly a year, the dogs in the street had been barking about Brian Lenihan going around like a demented DIY enthusiast, sawing in turn at each of the legs of the bockety table in an effort to stop it wobbling. And the cats on the other side of the street had been gleefully screeching back that soon the table would have no legs at all.

So George, once in power, would – what? – cancel the levies and restore the Christmas bonus? George didn't say. He merely went on to remind everyone that he had been the boy who said that the emperor had no clothes. He had 'spoken directly and impartially' to people as clearly as he could. As danger loomed, he had 'consistently highlighted the risks of inaction and complacency'. But his warnings were ignored. Actually, no, George decided, the government had chosen to portray his impartial and clear messages as 'an effort to talk down the economy'. It sounded as if George wanted to get them all back for being mean about him.

George seemed clear in his mind that we needed to get the country 'back on track' and that this could not be done with the present lot in power. That is why he wanted to offer 'in a small way' the change and the leadership the country needed.

But, when you rummaged through the wrapping in search of George's solutions, all that seemed to be there was George's intense belief in his own abilities and insights.

He said that, if we wanted to put things to rights, the best thing was for him to become part of the Fine Gael team and get elected as a TD for Dublin South. It was clear to him that Fine Gael under Enda Kenny was the party best placed to provide the kind of leadership and vision the country needed.

George won the by-election to much fanfare. The people of Ireland smiled for the first time in many months, and then went back to work and waited for the revolution.

Nothing happened, and this nothingness was followed by more of the same. Eight months later, George emerged, virtually in tears, from a broom cupboard he had been given in a building on Kildare Street. Nobody would listen to him, he said. Nobody cared what he thought about anything. He was in total disagreement with Fine Gael party policy and nobody gave a toss. Everyone was still being mean to him. George ran screaming out into Kildare Street, saying he was jacking it all in and returning to his job in RTE.

George Lee's experience tells us many things about the deep malaise at the heart of Irish politics. It illustrates the madness that arises from the absence of true idealism in the Irish body politic that a man known only for being paid to criticize economic policy can come to be seen as a national redeemer. But it also highlights the cynicism of politicians who think they can use such a figure to give the impression of vision where none exists, and also perhaps the vulnerability of journalists to the power of their own delusions. It took about a year for the complete George Lee drama to unfold. The only thing that changed, in the end, was that George had a free space for life in the Leinster House car park.

48 Brian Cowen

In May 2008, when Brian Cowen replaced Bertie Ahern as Taoiseach, the national mood was one of increasingly fragile denial. Within months, media commentators would come to describe the new Taoiseach as a disaster, the worst ever. But, for now, the talk was all about his unparalleled intelligence, his history of toughness on the football field, the fact that he could hold a pint or ten and sing a song in the snug of any public house in which the gauntlet was thrown down.

Deeper still, the implication of such commentary was that we were still on the hog's back. What we needed was another affable actor to maintain the mood of the previous decade. To suggest otherwise might have been to acknowledge what was already known in the bones of the culture: that we were in deep trouble.

Cowen, as Minister for Finance over several years, and as a core member of the team that had been running the country since 1997, was unquestionably centrally responsible for the situation faced by the Irish economy in 2008: the failures, for example, to understand what had been happening in the banking sector, or to alert the public to the disaster that threatened them.

In good times, Brian Cowen had seemed an effective number two, but there was scant evidence that he had either the charisma or the vision for the top job. His much-vaunted intelligence had yet to be demonstrated in any significant context beyond the party rooms, but had become an off-the-peg cliché to be lobbed into articles about the new Taoiseach by journalists who would later turn on Cowen with a vengeance rarely encountered in Irish political commentary.

Almost immediately after Cowen's coronation as Fianna Fáil leader and Taoiseach, the excrement started hitting the extractor. If, previously, we had indulgently regarded Bertie Ahern as a bit of a jammy dodger, then it became increasingly obvious that we hadn't known the half of it. Almost to the minute, he seemed to have timed his departure to coincide with the end of the good times. If Bertie had stayed another three months, which would have been long enough for enough of the facts to emerge, Cowen might have had a chance of being seen as the new broom come to clean up the mess. Then again, nobody really believed it was pure accident that Bertie, the jammy dodger to bury all jammy dodgers, got to leave in his blaze of martyred glory just before the pipe began to spew forth bad news, followed by worse.

Cowen made a serious mistake in agreeing to be crowned without a contest, ensuring that he was not required to set out a leadership stall. This sowed seeds of resentment among the public, which before long began to ask why it should have to accept as its leader someone with whom it had never developed a relationship.

Soon, as the awful reality began to roll out, the national mood came to resemble that extended instant just after you've had a prang at the traffic lights, when, as you get out of the car in slow motion to survey the damage, you think, 'I don't need this; therefore it can't be happening.' At such moments, there is a sensation of being lost in time, of feeling, against the apparent facts, that the past is still recoverable, though the future is already making itself clear.

The appalling suddenness of events seemed to insinuate that it was possible to go back in time and erase the whole thing, to wake up from the nightmare. The rhetoric of the previous decade had so convinced people that we had finally emerged from the mists of history and penury that this could only be a terrible nightmare. The utter unfairness of it all seemed to render the circumstances momentarily implausible, and therefore redeemable. But then reality reasserted itself. The facts started to sink in.

The Taoiseach and his ministers began to break the bad news – at first gently and then rather more forcefully. But their words were utterly incapable of penetrating the public mindset. Cowen and his cabinet seemed to be banking on a residual public memory of the 1987 Ray MacSharry cutbacks, retrospectively credited with rescuing the Irish economy and laying the foundations for the subsequent boom. But that had been two decades before, when half the 2008 electorate had yet to be born. And for those who remembered the 1980s, this new crisis seemed of an entirely different order.

Cowen just didn't seem to know what to do about anything. In one speech he would try to upbraid the public for not grasping how serious things were; in another he would declare that everything was really okay. One moment he seemed to be blaming the World Bank and the IMF for having validated mistaken decisions made in the good times; the next he was citing the approval of these same institutions for decisions being made about turning the economy around.

In as far as a strand of thought could be identified, the government's thinking was clearly more focused on preserving the image of our political class on the world stage than with securing the future for Irish children yet unborn. Because of his personality and the way he came to lead, nobody had any confidence in anything Cowen proposed to do. Everybody struggled against the twisting of fate. Precious time was lost. The problems grew worse. By the time the Minister for Finance, Brian Lenihan, finally unveiled his package to save the banking system, there had been a slippage of €10 million from his original estimate of the damage.

There was a strange sense that these unprecedented initiatives, which threatened the long-term future of Irish society, were being implemented because nobody was prepared to spell out the full extent of the situation. It was pointed out by some commentators that this was not the first time a country had been in a situation like this, and many of the options being brushed aside by Cowen and his cabinet had already worked elsewhere. For example, there was nothing crazy about the idea, proposed by a number of eminent economists, of temporarily pulling out of the euro. There was something deeply sane about the idea of leaving the banks to sink or swim in the consequences of their own recklessness. But not merely did Cowen not consider such ideas – even as a way of opening up a potentially liberating public discussion – he treated them with a silent disdain that suggested they had no merit at all. There were radical options available from the outset, but Brian Cowen was not the man to implement them. But he and his Minister for Finance, Brian Lenihan, valued international financial respectability above all other values.

The really frightening thing was this absence of dialogue. Cowen behaved like a sullen parent on a rained-off picnic – refusing to explain or discuss things in their broader significance. The common-sensical questions of either eminent economists or the man and woman in the street found no purchase in the corridors of power.

Was it, for example, really axiomatic that, in the midst of global financial meltdown, when half the Irish population has acquired debts rooted in nothing but banking science fiction, a generation of Irish workers had to face lives of penury and pain? Why, if the crisis arose from a dysfunctional banking system, must the banks be accorded every assistance to escape from the mess they'd created for themselves, while the ordinary citizen was to be hammered for his minor part in the same mess?

History will almost certainly decide that perhaps the greatest damage wrought by Brian Cowen resulted from a lack of courage, imagination and radicalism. The absence of these characteristics sprang, really, from a personality forged out of small-town values, and driven by, above all, a longing for respectability.

The truth is that Brian Cowen was never cut out to be a leader of anything more demanding than a football team. Entering a time of national emergency, the citizens of the Republic woke up one morning to find at their head, without being able to remember quite how or why it had happened, a Taoiseach who was elected on the basis that he was a helluva nice fella and it was his turn to wear the captain's jersey.

49 Enda Kenny

The problem with Enda Kenny is that he came to the leadership of Fine Gael because nobody else really wanted it as much as he did. There was a desultory contest with four candidates, but Kenny came out on top in the secret ballot because he was the most affable and best organized of the contenders. As a former chief whip, he was well known to all members of the Fine Gael parliamentary party and was more popular than the others. He had been an unsuccessful candidate just eighteen months before, when he was defeated by Michael Noonan.

The party had 'lost' three leaders in the previous decade or so – first Alan Dukes, then John Bruton and finally Noonan, a cartoonish figure from Limerick who had been made famous in Dermot Morgan's depiction in the weekly radio satirical show, *Scrap Saturday*. In the case of each of the three previous leaders, there had been a sense of entitlement. It has long been clear that either Dukes or Bruton was destined to become the successor to Garret FitzGerald, so each took his turn and each was dispatched following poor election results. Dukes and Bruton were both removed by internal coups, while Noonan stepped down before the same fate could befall him.

Kenny was to become a kind of default leader, having been elected after the party had lost the will to live. He had been a moderately impressive trade and tourism minister in John Bruton's Rainbow cabinet. Everyone liked him. He was good fun, smart and idealistic in a commonsense kind of way. But nobody thought about him as leadership material until he suddenly got the idea into his head. There were suggestions that the notion had been implanted by his wife, Fionnuala O'Kelly, who had been a press officer for Charles Haughey, and had crossed the tribal line to marry the young teacher from Mayo.

From the party's perspective, the choice of Kenny as leader was motivated by a desire, at a time of unprecedented economic prosperity, to clone the 'Bertie factor' by choosing someone with a high affability quotient to compete with Bertie Ahern for the feel-good sentiment that seemed destined to last forever.

For years, Enda Kenny had been a boon companion to political cronies and journalists in the network of pubs in the vicinity of Leinster House. As a party piece, he would deliver from the political speeches by John F. Kennedy, in a convincing imitation of the original. He was funny, decent and thoughtful.

But, as a leader, Kenny was beset by a problem. Seeming to lack the confidence to claim the authority of leadership, he began to act out the role. He was not so much Enda Kenny, Taoiseach-in-waiting, as Enda Kenny playing Enda Kenny in the role of Taoiseach-in-waiting.

As a political organizer and backslapper, Kenny had few equals. He did amazing work, scraping Fine Gael off the floor and putting it back into contention. At a grassroots level he was liked and respected, mainly because he had no airs or graces about him.

Early on in his leadership, some newspapers tried to label him a racist on account of a joke he had told at a party gathering. There was much huffing and puffing about whether, 'in a multicultural society', Kenny could be a suitable Taoiseach. It was nonsense. All that had happened was that the old Enda had briefly resurfaced in what he imagined might be a safe environment. He had used the word 'nigger' in a story about being on a junket to some African country some years before, when a black barman had used the word. It was not a good joke, but only an idiot would have adduced it as evidence that Enda was a racist.

It was after this that the iron seemed to enter his soul. He would not tell any more stories. He would not make any more jokes. He would not be himself, because this was too dangerous. As party leader, he became ponderous and heavy-handed. He acquired from someplace a deep, mellifluous voice, full of sound and fury. He began to use his hands in a statesmanlike way and generally tried to project himself as a serious phenomenon. He seemed to reach deep into himself to find unplumbed depths of pomposity before delivering himself of an opinion, a witticism or a condemnation. Nobody could take it seriously. He became the butt of routines by every two-bit comedian in the land. They called him 'the ginger whinger', 'the stiff with the quiff', or 'Endaman'.

All this was very unfair. Anyone who had talked to Kenny at any length knew him to be an immensely thoughtful man with a host of good ideas about how Irish society should function. That this has failed to come across is in part due to his personality, which has an element of shyness, and in part to the way he has been persuaded to present himself by those advising him about 'media skills'.

There was much more to Kenny than this, but almost nothing of his undoubted thoughtfulness was coming across. Instead, what impressed itself on the public mind was a charicature who made exaggerated rhetorical interjections in the style of the *múinteoir scoile* playing a parish priest in an amateur dramatics production of a play written by the local garda sergeant.

One day in late 2009, Enda Kenny seemed to wake up deciding

to become Garret FitzGerald. In his presidential address to a party gathering, Enda seemed to launch not so much a new initiative as a new version of himself: more decisive, more presidential, intent upon slaying sacred cows. He was embarking on – although he did not use the term – a constitutional crusade, proposing to abolish the Seanad and do God knew what else. That Monday morning, Enda fetched up on *Morning Ireland* to talk about his 'leader's initiative'. In the course of an eight-minute interview, Enda used the word 'I' forty-five times, and, perhaps more tellingly, the words 'Fine Gael' just once, as in 'it's not beyond the bounds of possibility that the Fine Gael party will form a government on its own'. The Irish people shuddered at the thought. But Enda's message seemed to be less about the Seanad than about the decisiveness and leadership qualities of Enda Kenny. 'What I offer,' he declared, 'is leadership, experience and change.'

Soon afterwards, Kenny took a drubbing in a series of media interviews. In one such interview it became clear that he was a little woolly about his own party's policy on water charges. Then he went on *The Late Late Show* and assured Ryan Tubridy that he knew 'who Harry Potter is'. The people of Ireland groaned and wept.

A few weeks later, he took another hammering, when George Lee, Kenny's parachutist candidate from RTE, who stormed to a famous victory in a by-election in Dublin South, resigned from politics because he had been ignored by the party leadership. Enda went on the radio and announced that, from here on out, he was going to be himself. Enough already, said the people of Ireland.

During an attempted coup in the summer of 2010, Kenny's stalwart band of loyalists successfully put about the suggestion that the rebels were a bunch of prissy capuccino drinkers, whereas Kenny's people were people of the soil and ate their dinners in the middle of the day. It worked and Kenny survived. But the problem with Enda Kenny is not a matter of city-slicker snobbery, it is that most people, from city and country, tay and cappuccino drinkers alike, think he is a terrible eejit. Whether it is true or fair, is neither here not there. In fact, it is almost certainly not true, but it sometimes appears to be true, and that is enough to make Enda Kenny an electoral liability while he remains leader of Fine Gael. Fine Gaelers keep saying Kenny has never lost an election, but this raises the troubling question as to why he is not already Taoiseach.

Kenny's primary problem is that he is outside mainstream Irish society looking in, rather than comfortably sitting within the changed and still changing Ireland and speaking on its behalf. He is the product of smokefilled party backrooms rather than the street sensibility of a country in which everything clicks a hundred times snappier than when he entered politics thirty-five years ago. This changed Ireland is waiting for new faces and voices who would effortlessly respond to the mood and tenor of the Now. Kenny is not alone – nor even the worst offender – but he is in the awkward position of seeming set to become Ireland's leader for most of the next decade.

At a time when the country had plumbed depths of despair beyond anything in living memory, when belief in the incumbent government was at rock bottom, it should have been easy for the opposition to gain public confidence and approval. To an extent, Fine Gael did pick up some of the slack arising from the broken faith in Fianna Fáil. But, given the extent of the crisis, much more might have been expected to happen. There might have been mass candlelight demonstrations filling O'Connell Street after dark. There might have been a storming of government buildings. The reason none of this happened is that everyone looked from Brian Cowen to Enda Kenny and asked themselves, 'What's the point?'

Instead, silently, microscopically in every citizen's heart, there began the gradual diminution of hope. We could talk as much as we liked, but no matter what we did, short of an armed coup, there was no prospect of real change. We were faced with a stark and comfortless choice: that everything might get gradually worse under Brian Cowen, or that we would wake up one morning to be told that it was not a question of what our country could do for us, but what we could do for our country.

50 Thierry Henry

For nearly a thousand years, the English did their utmost to grind the Irish into the dust. For the best part of a century in the wake of independence, the Irish seemed to be attempting to complete that project. But then, one night in November 2009, a dark-skinned Frenchman, employing to deadly effect his left hand, finally landed the killer blow.

After fifteen months of unremitting misery, in which the Irish people had observed their hopes of material well-being melt before their eyes, there had been just the slimmest possibility of a place in the World Cup Finals. This would have been much more than a sporting achievement. We Irish were not exactly accustomed to winning things, but we had some good memories of coming third or fourth. Moreover, such sporting adventures always seemed, when seen in retrospect anyway, to awaken in the Irish psyche something deeper and more resilient. The idea that the seeds of the Celtic Tiger germinated during Italian 90, when Ireland almost made it to the semi-finals, is impossible to shift from the Irish orbifrontal cortex. All this rendered that night in November 2009 an episode beyond tragedy and pathos.

When Thierry Henry brought that ball under control with his hand and slipped it into the Irish net, he was bringing to an end not just the hopes of a team and its followers, but the hopes of an entire nation who saw this as a final sign from the gods.

Sometimes, when you have overcome a deep resistance to optimism and found your fortunes improving, you begin to imagine that perhaps the psychobabblers are right when they say that failure and success are all in the mind. In the early years of the Celtic Tiger, people who retained memories of previous false dawns followed by renewed misfortune, had held their optimism in check. By the early years of the new millennium, most of us were beginning to let our hair down, overcoming our pessimism to embrace this new and, we were persuaded, permanent sunshine. No sooner had we done so, however, than the clouds started to gather again, and we found this as hard to credit as we had the idea that hardship and want had been consigned to the past. We hadn't rushed into things, but when we did embrace the new dispensation, we did so wholeheartedly and with abandon, and now we were having to face the possibility that our pessimism had offered the best counsel after all.

Many still harboured hopes that the whole thing had been a mistake, that one day soon we would all wake up and find that we were still on the pig's back. But Henry's goal put an end to all that – more because of its unfairness than the effect it had on the scoreline. Afterwards, he was a little sheepish but still clearly uncomprehending of the incoherent rage directed at him by the Irish. He was not to know that he had just confirmed for many Irish people that the hind tit was our only reliable and consistent recourse. Life was not fair, at least not to us. We might have cheated the facts for a while, but it had all been a mistake. The good fortune had been, as our deepest intuition had always whispered, intended for a different address. This was more like the normal run of events.

The desire for justice is instilled in every human heart, giving birth to an expectation of being treated fairly, which is to say 'the same as anyone else', or 'according to the rules', or by whatever other criteria this craving may be measured. But in the Irish personality, this natural desire for justice had long since been suppressed by a violent and abusive history in which fairness was to be found only in the colouring of my true love's hair. The Irish weather, too, has always exhibited a vengeful caprice which has instilled in the Irish soul a modest level of expectation of what tomorrow may being.

As a result of these pre-conditions, it had taken a lot for us to trust history again, and now we were being shown the folly of this grudging and cautious faith. Our natural sense of justice having been restored by a decade of good fortune, we were as ill-equipped for Thierry Henry's handball as we were for a return of Oliver Cromwell.

And when an injustice occurs which inflicts on the human being's constitutive sense of justice a blow that seems to be both arbitrary and unfair, the resulting sense of metaphysical outrage breaks free of all language and becomes a kind of deep, inner scream. This, in slow motion, is what happened in the days following the Henry outrage.

For more than an hour on that Wednesday night it had looked like Ireland was in with a chance of playing in the World Cup in South Africa. In the depths of recession, this prospect carried with it an enhanced significance, having the potential to lift the spirit of the nation out of the fatalism that has dogged it for eighteen months. The dashing of these hopes, by something widely acknowledged to be unfair, had therefore the potential to provoke in the Irish psyche a twist that threatened permanent damage.

It was made worse by the fact that nobody, not even the French, disputed the unfairness of it all. Thus, at an emotional level, the handball issue offered a simplified version of the infinitely more complicated equation to be observed in the economic context. If everyone could see it was a handball; if the French press and public overwhelmingly thought the French team stole the game, then the solution seemed obvious and simple. But then we noticed that, although everyone was paying lip-service to Irish grief, nobody was actually suggesting that anything be done to put the matter to rights.

This resonated deeply with feelings surfacing in the economic arena. France's qualification on the back of Henry's cynical opportunism provoked the same intensity of rage as government bail-outs for bankers who had created massive inflation in house prices, ultimately provoking the crash. In both instances, the beneficiaries of cheating were seen to sail onwards, immune from consequences, while the punters were blithely told that, yes, it's unfair, but there is nothing to be done. Rules is rules, you know. The winners shook their heads and said how sheepish they felt, but still booked their trips to the sun. Just as FIFA officials intoned that the referee is the final arbiter, those in charge of the economy insisted that, notwithstanding the clear ethical and regulatory breaches at the heart of the banking crisis, there was no possibility of moral redress.

It seemed that, sometime about eighteen months before, the gods changed their mind about us. Before that, we had soaked in a veritable Jacuzzi of good fortune, experiencing a rising tide of prosperity, optimism and occasional sporting success. But then, practically overnight, without any announcement being made, a shift had occurred. Already, it was clear, the plug had been pulled on the economy. Now, it seemed, the sporting successes were suspended until further notice.

If you hadn't lived through the Celtic Tiger, you might not have understood the mood of the previous eighteen months. And if you hadn't shared in the hope of those two hours on that night in November, you might have had difficulty in understanding the ructions that followed. When you put the two phenomena together, you were forced to the conclusion that fate had again taken to dealing us the same unkind hand in everything. Ireland going out of the World Cup after a brief resurgence of hope could, in this light, be seen not just as an ordinary misfortune, but as a second bereavement following hard on one we had not yet come to terms with.

The Irish wept and gnashed their teeth, but it was the French who were going to South Africa. And as they wept and wailed, the Irish people began to enter into a sense of themselves and their historical condition that many of them had imagined had been left behind for ever. Something about the experience of this unfairness was familiar. It was as if there were songs about it already, but we had forgotten the words.